Changing Course

Changing Course

HEALING FROM LOSS, ABANDONMENT, AND FEAR

Claudia Black

Third Edition

CENTRAL RECOVERY PRESS

Las Vegas, Nevada

Central Recovery Press (CRP) is committed to publishing exceptional materials addressing addiction treatment, recovery, and behavioral healthcare topics.

For more information, visit www.centralrecoverypress.com.

Publisher: Central Recovery Press
3321 N. Buffalo Drive
Las Vegas, NV 89129

26 25 24 23 22 21   1 2 3 4 5

Library of Congress Cataloging-in-Publication Data
Names: Black, Claudia, author.
Title: Changing course : healing from loss, abandonment, and fear / Claudia
    Black, PhD.
Description: Third edition. | Las Vegas, NV : Central Recovery Press, 2021.
    | Summary: "Claudia Black extends a helping hand to individuals working
    their way through the painful experience of being raised with addiction
    in the family"-- Provided by publisher.
Identifiers: LCCN 2021014743 (print) | LCCN 2021014744 (ebook) | ISBN
    9781949481488 (paperback) | ISBN 9781949481495 (ebook)
Subjects: LCSH: Adult children of dysfunctional families. | Adjustment
    (Psychology) | Healing.
Classification: LCC RC455.4.F3 B527 2021 (print) | LCC RC455.4.F3 (ebook)
    | DDC 616.89/156--dc23
LC record available at https://lccn.loc.gov/2021014743
LC ebook record available at https://lccn.loc.gov/2021014744

Photo of Claudia Black by Winifred Whitfield. Used with permission.

Publisher's Note
This book contains general information about mental health, family systems, familial roles, relationships, codependency, and trauma recovery. The information contained herein is not medical advice. This book is not an alternative to medical advice from your doctor or other professional healthcare provider.

Our books represent the experiences and opinions of their authors only. Every effort has been made to ensure that events, institutions, and statistics presented in our books as facts are accurate and up-to-date. To protect their privacy, the names of some of the people, places, and institutions in this book may have been changed.

Cover design and interior by Deb Tremper, Six Penny Graphics.

In memory of my dad,
Bill (Wilmer Dale) Clark

Table of Contents

A Note from the Author

Changing Course will offer you a framework to heal pain related to loss and abandonment and to better understand many things about your life. It will challenge you to reflect to a greater depth by answering pointed questions. My hope is that you will not only think about the questions but also write down your thoughts. Doing so leads to greater insight and revelations.

To begin, gather the writing utensils you favor and a notebook or journal that will be specific to this journey. I also want you to get a highlighter pen with transparent ink, such as yellow or pink. As you read, underline or mark the words and sentences that make you feel as if I am speaking directly to you.

As you answer the questions, allow yourself to write freely without being concerned about grammar or punctuation. The questions may churn up many feelings, so plan a safety net for yourself ahead of time. It may be helpful to have a private space in which you do your writing. Is there anyone you can share some of this experience with? Remember to take time to breathe deeply and pause if feelings arise and you feel overwhelmed. And do this your way. Some people prefer to answer the questions as they are reading. Others will answer the questions within a chapter when they come to the end of that chapter. If you prefer to read the entire book and go back to the questions, do so. And if the questions are too much, don't despair. A good book is read more than once. This is your journey to do at your pace.

Chapter One

Changing Course

Turning Points to Recovery

I don't know when my parents began their war against each other, but I do know the only prisoners they took were their children. When we needed to escape, we developed a ritual—we found a silent soothing world where there was no pain, a world without mothers and fathers. But that was a long time ago, before I chose not to have a memory.

—Pat Conroy

Forgiving is not forgetting. It is remembering and letting go.

—Claudia Black

I've spent my whole life trying to take the pain out of everyone else's life! The whole time, the issue was my pain, not theirs. Today I don't run scared. I know my fear, my hurt, my anger. I also know my joy. Today I don't live in shame.

—Lynn

Fear and loneliness were all I ever knew—I think I came into this world scared. But now, at forty-two, it's different. I have used most things—gambling, women, sex, alcohol—to medicate my fears and not feel so lonely. Today I no longer use people, activities, and substances to medicate or keep me separated from my feelings. I've slowed down to be able to meet myself. And I realize I am okay. I am more than okay! I actually look forward to each day.

—Joe

I wanted so badly to be loved, but for years all I felt was ignored and unwanted. I went to every length possible to make people love me, only to be repeatedly ignored and unwanted. Then, slowly, with the understanding of what had happened in my life and with the freedom to talk about it, things started to turn around. I learned to love myself. What a revelation!

—Sherie

These people endured decades of pain and then discovered a different way of being in this world, a different way of living their lives. Why did they have pain? How did it go away? What was their turning point? How did they change the course of their lives? These are some of the questions I will try to answer here.

When we grow up with fear and shame we become adults who live with fear and shame. Accompanying these intense feelings is a pervasive, chronic sense of loss, ranging anywhere from serious to profound. The sensation of this loss goes by various names: *unhappiness, hopelessness, depression, emptiness, insecurity, anxiety, boredom.* Whatever the words we use, these wounds have troubled our very spirit. We need to let go of the fear and shame. We need to change our course by putting the cause of our pain in its proper perspective.

What you might be feeling depends on what you felt when the original wounding began, compounded by your life experiences from that time on. It will be difficult to look back at those troubling times, but this is where your recovery begins.

For some of us, life in our early years was organized around our mother's drinking and the subsequent embarrassment and shame. Or our brother's death and the fear, stigma, and prevailing sadness we endured. Or our father's rigid religious fervor and the shame, confusion, guilt, and anger we felt. Or our parents' outright abandonment of their parenting roles and the ensuing abandonment of us, their children. Or our physical or sexual abuse by someone who was supposed to love us.

Early on, we were deprived of the very conditions necessary for us to thrive as children. We lost the opportunity to be ourselves. We lived as characters in someone else's drama, a story of his or her war against pain. The family spotlight was nearly always on that other person, and we were merely bit players, "lesser lights" whose characters were never developed in the family script. The lines we were supposed to speak and our range of emotions were limited so that we didn't conflict with the main character who, in essence, stole the show.

Many of us accept the idea of chronic loss, but we can't put our finger on any specific event that was the cause of that loss. Perhaps there was no identifiable abuse, addiction, or other blatant dysfunction in our lives. In our case, the loss was growing in the shadow of our parents' pain. Factoring in what we know now, we would probably see that our parents had been character actors in someone else's play. In many ways, the other play is still going on off-stage in the wings of our lives. As a result, what happened in our families was far less obvious, but we were affected nonetheless.

Regardless of how subtle or blatant the pain was in a family, we learned to push our concerns aside and stuff our feelings away.

Living by the Rules

Don't Talk, Don't Trust, Don't Feel
I have this great job. I travel. I'm self-sufficient. Maybe I don't need to be able to get closer to people.

I'm fifty-two years old. Why should I be angry with my dad for being a victim of his era? All dads hit their kids once in a while. So my dad made bruises! My life isn't so bad.

My mother created a lot of pain in my life, being so critical and acting like a jealous girlfriend, but she was also all I had. It could have been worse.

There are always other people who have had greater difficulty, more pain in their lives; the fact that others had it worse doesn't take away your loss. There will always be a greater horror story. Your loss is not negated by someone else's. Your loss is your own pain.

How do you go from living according to the rules—Don't Talk, Don't Trust, Don't Feel—to a life where you are free to talk and trust and feel?

You do this through a process that teaches you to go to the source of those old, transgenerational rules, to question them and to recreate new rules of your own. You will also have to grieve what is now in the past but is still painful. You will discover that your life will change course as a result of this process of renewal.

Going Back to the Past

My friends have given me all the books, but I don't want to touch those issues.

I'm twenty-three. I want to move on in my life. I don't want to go back to it.

Why would I want to talk about that now? It was a long time ago.

People who resist going back to face difficult childhood issues are not fully acknowledging the pain of the loss or trauma that occurred in their lives. For many people it has become easier to develop defenses to avoid facing their pain—process or substance addictions, disordered eating, perfectionism or extreme caretaking, for instance. These behaviors are often culturally supported. They anesthetize pain and possibly offer esteem. All of this causes people to question why they should want to change.

While you can't relive those early years, you can recover from the pain of the past—gradually. Little by little, you can let down those defenses that once helped you survive but are actually hurting you now. You can learn new life skills so you can begin to accept and internalize that it is truly possible for you
    to be imperfect and still be lovable;
    make mistakes and still be accepting of yourself; and
    feel and express your feelings openly, honestly, safely.

No more secret shame. No more need to make a superhuman effort to stay in control so you can keep up appearances. No more need to protect your vulnerability and hide your true self from others. No more need to put up barriers that keep people at a distance.

This new way of living is possible for those who choose it—whenever they choose it. Young, middle-aged, or older, recovery is there if you want it. Recovery starts with recognizing that you would like at least part of your life to be different than it is now.

The turning point in your life comes with a new awareness:

ᕼ "There is another reality than the one I live. I want it."

Then a new willingness:

ᕼ "I am willing to take some risks to have it."

This book offers a framework for understanding the recovery/healing process from childhood family pain that has been carried forward in your life. It will help you to understand the beliefs and behaviors that have perpetuated your pain. It will identify specific steps in recovery, examine the core issues you will face, and offer guidelines regarding expectations for yourself and others you care about.

All of our lives can be viewed on a continuum from "No Pain" to "All Pain," and the combined effect of our experiences, past and present, falls somewhere between these extremes. There is no amount you must have suffered in order to have permission to heal.

ᕼ If you have pain, you deserve to heal.

ᕼ If you have anger or guilt from the past, you deserve to heal.

ᕼ If you are protecting yourself from past pain in ways that are causing you even more pain in the present, you deserve to heal.

At birth, a child has a "bill of human rights." Children have the right
• to be loved for who they are rather than for being what others wish them to become;

- to be nurtured and parented rather than to make up for their parents' losses;
- to have consistency, security, warmth, and understanding;
- to have unconditional love; and
- to be protected from traumatic situations.

Yet, for children raised in troubled families, these basic rights are lost. Instead, they must struggle for the right merely to survive. As a consequence of their loss, these adult-age individuals have difficulty experiencing a healthy life until the child within each of them is able to speak the truth about childhood and get free from the bondage of the past. Until this recognition and healing occurs, people are subject to live a life without choice, reliving old pain and controlling the pain in hurtful ways. Unless something changes, they are characters trapped in their old life dramas, destined to live out old scripts.

❖ *Reflect on the* statement: "At birth a child has a bill of rights." How strongly do you agree or disagree with this statement?

Chronic Loss and Abandonment

A family's life together is troubled when the conditions that foster physical and emotional growth and well-being are continuously absent over time. The absence of these nurturing conditions has the cumulative effect of creating a childhood experience of chronic loss and abandonment. Within a family, the dynamics that create a sense of loss are denial, rigidity, emotional isolation, and shame. Everyone will experience these things occasionally, but when children experience any of these four factors to a severe degree they carry forward an overriding sense of chronic loss.

Some Loss Is Necessary; Some Is Not
We all experience loss in life. From birth we embark on a journey of separation from our fathers and mothers. The losses we experience are natural or necessary losses and are balanced by gains that build our strength and health.

Children naturally experience loss of some level of security as they enter school. There is a sense of loss when children move to a new area and a new home. They experience another kind of natural loss through the death of a loved one, most apt at that age to be a grandparent. Another common natural loss is that of a pet. This is a painful time and often a child's first experience with death. As painful as that can be, it is less so in our father's or mother's arms.

In a troubled family, children are often not supported in their pain or are told not to show what they feel. Sometimes they're also told not to feel what they feel—to keep a stiff upper lip, to stop crying, to stop acting like a child. In a severely dysfunctional family, the scenario might be that one parent intentionally causes the loss—for example, by giving away the child's cat—and the other parent denies the significance of what happened, maybe even denies that it happened at all. When we experience a natural loss and are supported by our parents we feel sad but loved and secure. When we are not supported we feel sad, unloved, abandoned. This lack of support or help with our pain is an abandonment experience.

Abandonment Is Not a Necessary Loss

Oh sure, I remember the first day of school. Don't we all? My seven-year-old sister woke me up yelling. She dressed me while Mom was sleeping. Dad was away. She held my hand, took me to her school, and told me to stay away from the older kids and not to fall asleep.

Two different times growing up my father actually gave our dogs away—they were my best friends. My parents told us both times that they were killed by cars, but I overheard Mom telling Grandma the real story.

I remember my graduation. My dad was too busy to get there until it was over.

These are examples of children who were emotionally abandoned. They were not offered solace, direction, or support at significant times in their lives. They were not offered protection at times of natural loss; many of them may even have been in families that created losses for children. What is most damaging is that these losses take place at the time in life when children are developing their self-worth.

The losses are most often due to emotional abandonment, physical abandonment, or a combination of the two.

Emotional abandonment occurs when the parent or primary caretaker is not emotionally available to the child on a consistent basis. While physical needs are possibly being met, there is little or no nurturing, hugging, or emotional intimacy developing between the parent and the child. The unnecessary losses a child experiences may range from loss of quality and quantity of time with a parent, loss of childhood as a result of unrealistic expectations placed on the child, loss of hope, loss of opportunity, to loss of innocence.

By the time I was seven, I was the little adult at home. I had to be perfect. There was no laughter, no fun, no tenderness.

After my third foster home, I knew no one was coming for me.

My dad didn't care about me. He clearly liked being away from home better than he liked us kids. By the time I was eleven, I didn't care much about things either. No one had time for me, so what did it matter if I was a screw up?

Loss is not always a result of what does happen; sometimes, loss is the result of what does *not* happen. Maybe you had a need that went unnoticed. Maybe you did not hear a parent say, "I love you" or "You are special." The loss could also be a result of what you didn't get to say because your parents weren't available, or what you didn't get to do with them, such as play or work on projects. Words and time are important to all children as they grow up. They convey to us that we are valued.

Physical abandonment occurs when a child has repetitively missed meals, has been left alone for hours or days unsupervised, or has been left without adequate supervision. Due to our ability to deny, we sometimes negate our abandonment. "I was always supervised. Maybe Mom and Dad weren't home, but my older brother was." Although being left with older siblings for lengthy periods of time may illustrate one child's valiant effort to protect another child, it still constitutes abandonment by parents. In spite of the maturity of our nine-, twelve-, or fifteen-year-old siblings, they are still nine, twelve, or fifteen. We needed adult supervision and protection. Not being properly clothed or not having physical protection are forms of abandonment. Any acts of physical and sexual abuse are forms of physical abandonment. It is an act of physical abandonment when the child is treated as an object and not as a person. Those who are responsible for you owe it to you to see that you are not violated. You deserve protection. Not feeling secure, protected, safe—both psychologically and physically—creates the greatest loss for children. The messages heard by the child experiencing emotional abandonment and physical abandonment are very similar: "You are not of value; you are not wanted; you are in the way."

Being in a family where there is chronic loss is traumatic; it gravely interferes with our ability to feel good about ourselves and the world. It can interfere with developing skills that lead to connecting and bonding. It will be significant in the creation of internalized fear and shame.

Denial

Denial is a defense mechanism, a natural response to protect against pain. When we feel helpless to impact our situation or ashamed of what is occurring, we often resort to denial. Denial can be identified when individuals discount, minimize, or rationalize their feelings. As a nine-year-old put it, "Denial is pretending things are different than how they really are." While the word *denial* is most often associated with the addictive family, it is the central dynamic of any dysfunctional system.

To be raised with denial is to know the Rule of Silence. As children, we learned that it was not okay to speak our truth and, instead, we should pretend things were different than they were. It may be that our perceptions were not validated, or we felt threatened about speaking up for fear of the consequences or punishment. We may have felt hopeless, believing that nothing good would come from talking. As children raised with the Rule of Silence, we became confused about loyalty. Often we didn't speak up because we were afraid we wouldn't be believed. As upset, frightened, or concerned as we were, we believed that we would jeopardize our well-being and betray those we loved if we spoke our truth.

If we were raised with others close to us also subscribing to the Rule of Silence, we had no practice trusting that those we spoke to would hear us. Many of us just didn't know what to say. We couldn't make sense of people's behavior. We didn't understand or know what was really happening, and we had no language to describe it. What we knew most were our feelings, and it was made clear to us that we weren't supposed to talk about them.

Growing up with denial makes it easy to be in denial today—and not know it. We discount our feelings and perceptions. We rationalize hurtful behaviors. Today, we may say we aren't angry, disappointed, or hurt when we are. We tell ourselves something isn't important when it is. We even tell ourselves certain things don't happen much when they occur frequently. We don't speak our truth. When we spend years learning to minimize, discount, or rationalize, it's only normal to continue to do so as adults. We are so skilled in denying that we do it without conscious thought.

■ *Consider reflecting on* the family in which you were raised and make a list of the things you could easily talk about. Make a list of those subjects it was not okay to talk openly about.

Rigidity

In troubled families parents are often dogmatic in their thinking: *Things will be this way and there are no exceptions.* The old adage, "Children are to be seen and not heard" is often adhered to. Inherent in this stance are the Don't Question and Don't Think rules. This is a family where it is never okay to challenge authority, and under the guise of respect you are to quietly submit.

Often, the rigidity is evident in the structure that is imposed on the children. There may be a lack of fairness regarding family rules and expectations. Parents are unrealistic, expecting far too much from their children. Their expectations aren't age-appropriate, such as expecting a six-year-old to do what is normal for a twelve-year-old. While children need consistency, rigid controls are discouraging and debilitating. "We weren't allowed out of the house outside of school and church. We couldn't have friends over. We always had chores or had to be doing schoolwork even when there was none to do." Not only is this rigidity often isolating for a child, but typically there are no rewards for the child who obeys. There is little likelihood the child is ever celebrated. To obey is an expectation; to perform is a requirement. In time the child finds no joy, feels the pain of isolation and, ultimately, if the child does not succumb to depression, the child will find hurtful ways in which to act out.

As a consequence of growing up with rigidity, we as adults are often rigid in our thinking. We have difficulty perceiving choices. We are unrealistic with ourselves and others, setting ourselves or others up to "never be good enough." We cannot find joy in our accomplishments. Or, we rebel and take on a permissive attitude with ourselves, often resulting in difficulty with being accountable and responsible.

> ✂ ***If you identify*** with being raised in a rigid family system, describe the impact it has had on you.

Isolation

Emotional isolation is also a common experience for children in troubled families. Isolation is particularly damaging because we need a connection with others to create meaning in life. Yet we live life as if in a bubble, shouting, "Hello out there—I'm alive in here! Does anybody hear me?" But no one answers.

We have learned to live with emotional isolation as a result of not being able to speak our truth. Shelley, age thirteen, depicts the isolation we know so well. When asked to draw a picture of her home, she showed her bedroom and the living room amplified in size. In the living room, the parents were portrayed as being in a heated argument; there were footprints running from the living room to a bedroom where you then saw Shelley and her two sisters hiding at opposite ends of the room from each other behind separate beds. Even in crisis, the sisters were unable to connect, to bond, to be of support to each other.

The emotional isolation within the home often carries over to those outside of the family as well. We don't want others to know of our personal pain or the family pain. We are afraid of how others would respond if they knew. As adults we have come to be socially isolated, or we surround ourselves with others while withholding our true feelings and thoughts. The family rules, Don't Talk, Don't Trust, Don't Feel, create our isolation. While we may have social graces, our hallmark is superficiality.

> ❖ ***Draw a picture*** of the family in which you were raised that represents the closeness or lack of closeness you felt with the different family members.

Shame

Internalized shame becomes the foundation of a person's trauma. Shame is the painful feeling that comes with the belief there is something inherently wrong with who you are. It is the belief that you, or a part of you, is defective or inadequate. Words that describe shame are reflective of seeing oneself as "bad," "ugly," "stupid," "incompetent," "damaged."

To live with shame is to feel alienated and defeated, never quite good enough to belong. It is an isolating experience that makes us think we are completely alone and unique in our belief that we are unlovable. Secretly, we feel like we are to blame. Any and all deficiency lies within ourselves. Gershen Kaufman, author of *Shame: The Power of Caring,* said that "shame is without parallel, a sickness of the soul." Shame reflects an internal darkness in one's soul. And it is because of this our recovery truly has spiritual meaning.

Underneath layers of shame you will find that abandonment is at the foundation. Abandonment, as described earlier, may be emotional or physical. But abandonment is most often experienced through various forms of rejection, rejection that has been colored by parental words and actions, some subtle, some not so subtle. It is useful to visualize a continuum, with acceptance at one end, rejection at the other end, and many shades of emotional unavailability or parental indifference to your needs and wants somewhere between.

Emotional Abandonment

$$\text{Acceptance} \quad \frac{\text{Emotional Unavailability}}{\text{Indifference to Needs and Wants}} \quad \text{Rejection}$$

The in-between areas encompass the many ways a child can feel ignored or invalidated by the parents' nonaccepting or rejecting behaviors. Whether or not the parents' intention is abandonment, the child feels unloved and undervalued. And, remember, the child is reacting to parents whose job it is to protect, care for, and love him or her. If parents reject their children in any way, the children know in their hearts they must not be worthy.

> ✂ *Looking at the* Abandonment Line, note with a marker the degree to which you identify with emotional abandonment. The more you identify with acceptance or rejection, the closer your mark will be to that word.

No one's family is perfect; parents are people who, like everyone else, have vulnerabilities and faults. They often make mistakes. Nonetheless, anyone who has lived with chronic loss—loss resulting from a mixture of rigidity, denial, isolation, and shame—deserves the opportunity to heal.

How this loss is created is illustrated on the chart, "How Chronic Loss Is Created: The Experience of Pain from a Child's Point of View."

How Chronic Loss Is Created

The Experience of Pain from a Child's Point of View

Loss event occurs and/
or loss condition exists

Pain of loss felt by child

Attended   **Family responses to child's pain**   **Abandoned**

Child feels:
Comforted, cared for, allowed
permission to feel, reality of
loss validated, pain honored

Child feels:
Isolated, ignored, shamed,
blamed, reality of loss denied,
pain discounted, diminished.

Pain (grieved) (healed)

Pain of abandonment
added to pain of loss

**Child's reaction to
attended, healed pain**

Emotions	Beliefs
Safe	Okay
Protected	Worthy
Loved	Lovable
Connected	Guilt-Free

Behaviors
Open to being self, to expressing self.
Free of need for defensive, controlling
role.

**Child's reaction to
abandonment and loss pain**

Emotions	Beliefs
Fear	Shameful
Unprotected	Unworthy
Unloved	Unlovable
Isolated, alone	Guilty

Behaviors
Closed to being self; needs to
protect self. Tries to look good, seem
lovable. Plays role to defend self, to
control/"fix" family: Responsible One,
Placater, Adjuster, Acting-Out One.

**Attended Child's Family
Environment**
Free to thrive
Sense of self developed
Boundaries developed, strengthened

**Abandoned Child's
Family Environment**
Struggle to survive
Sense of self undeveloped
Boundaries vague, violated

Pain of loss + pain of abandonment = an abandonment experience

Chronic abandonment experiences = chronic loss

CHRONIC LOSS for a child = loss of conditions for thriving

The Impact of Our Losses

It is not possible to live with the dynamics of chronic loss and not be affected. While families have many common characteristics, there are all kinds of experiences that create differences. Some of these experiences impact us more negatively than others. There are many variables that create differences in the ways and the depth we feel the effects.

- Age at onset of trauma or loss. The younger we are, the more hurtful it is to us.
- Stigma associated to dynamics. If negative judgments are attached to our experiences, there are greater emotional consequences, i.e., there is greater stigma being in an abusive family than a home characterized by work addiction.
- Connection to outside support system. Connection to extended family, friend's family, extracurricular school activities, the ability to find meaningful relationships and/or activities outside of family lessens our shame.
- Multiple trauma-/shame-related dynamics. For example, to live with both addiction and abuse is more traumatic than to live with just one source of pain.

Usually about this stage in reading there is a tendency to begin saying to yourself, "Yes, but . . .": "Yes, but my dad wasn't all bad; he did do some good things in his parenting" or "Yes, but my mother did teach me . . ." or "Yes, but I love my dad." In spite of any loss or pain in one's growing-up years, we were given gifts by our parents. Those gifts will be ours to cherish. There is no doubt that we come from families with a matrix of strengths and vulnerabilities.

It is also clear that the survival skills we developed helped to create important personal strengths. To bring about greater predictability in our young lives and defend against the pain, we developed ways of coping that may have brought a resourcefulness to our personalities.

Yet we need to be cautious that we do not reinstate the Don't Talk or Don't Question rules by discounting the pain, all for the sake of recognizing how strong we are. Please recognize that owning the pain that occurred in your life in no manner lessens the gifts you were given and the strengths you have developed.

It is important to identify your losses. Until losses and pain are dealt with directly, the resulting feelings, while often masked, are carried into adulthood. Unless we have a chance to learn healthy coping skills, this combination of past loss and pain leads to severe consequences creating even more pain in the present.

> ✖ *To get a* more concrete picture of the losses in your life, it would be helpful for you to create a loss graph. See Appendix A for a Loss Graph form, with instructions, for you to record the losses in your early years.

Changing Course

To change course, be it a minor shift or a major turn in your life, does not mean giving up who you are—it means letting go of who you are not.

It means letting go of your pain. You are not your pain.

You will need to walk through the pain. However, you do not have to walk through the pain alone again as a helpless, vulnerable child. Remember, whatever you experienced as a child, your perceptions and interpretations were those of a child. The perceived belief that you were worthless or bad is not true. You never were bad or unworthy, and you are not today. It is my hope that, in time, you will be able to say and to believe in your heart, "I am good. I am adequate. I am worthy."

It means letting go of an undesirable family script. You are no longer an unwitting character in someone else's life now that you understand you have the freedom to choose.

Each insight into your past and its connection to your present is like turning on the light in a dark room. It doesn't change what is there, but now that you can see where you are going, you can go in and out freely without harm. Fear no longer drives you—freedom moves you.

Each of these awarenesses brings you new choices. Each new awareness is a turning point.

Chapter Two

You Can't Go Forward without Finishing the Past

Healing the Pain of Abandonment, Fear, and Shame

In this dream I was stationed underground, in the grave . . . This was my company, my life, my mission—to watch over the bones. And then slowly . . . I walked away and climbed out of the grave, into the sun and the wide expanse of the world . . . I turned one last time to say goodbye.

The vigil was over.

—John, adult child of an alcoholic

To free yourself from the past you must break the rules of silence and compliance.
—Claudia Black

When children are raised with chronic loss without the psychological or physical protection they need and certainly deserve, it is most natural for them to internalize incredible fear. Not receiving the necessary psychological or physical protection equals abandonment. And, living with repeated abandonment experiences creates shame. Shame arises from the painful message implied in abandonment: "You are not important. You are not of value." Unresolved pain of the past and pain in the present created by past-driven behaviors fuel our fear of abandonment and shame. This is the pain from which we need to heal.

Pain from the Past

Physical Abandonment
For some children abandonment is primarily physical. Physical abandonment occurs when the physical conditions necessary for thriving have been replaced by
- lack of appropriate supervision;
- inadequate provision of nutrition and meals;
- inadequate clothing, housing, heat, or shelter;
- physical abuse, which can include not just hitting but shoving, pushing, terrorizing car rides, etc.; and/or
- sexual abuse, which includes inappropriate touching, fondling, intercourse or anal sex, exposure to pornography, sex trafficking.

As children, we are totally dependent on our caretakers to provide safety in our environment. When they do not, we grow up believing that the world is an unsafe place, that people are not to be trusted, and that we do not deserve positive attention and adequate care.

▪ *Review the examples* of Physical Abandonment and circle any you identify with and/or name any that were not noted.

Emotional Abandonment
Emotional abandonment occurs when parents do not provide the emotional conditions and environment necessary for healthy development.

Because more people experience emotional abandonment than physical abandonment, and because it is a more subtle dynamic, the following experiences may be helpful to understanding emotional abandonment. There are two frameworks for abandonment that can simplify the term.

1. Abandonment is experienced by parental indifference to a child's needs and wants, or when parents (or other primary caregivers) are emotionally unavailable on an ongoing basis. They do not offer the support and nurturance a child needs. Therefore, the child can neither experience nor express his or her feelings appropriately.

2. Abandonment occurs when a child has to hide a part of who he or she is in order to be accepted or to protect themselves, such as when

   • It is not acceptable in your family to make a mistake.

   • It is not okay in your family to show feelings, being told the way you feel is not true or okay. "You have nothing to cry about, and if you don't stop crying I will really give you something to cry about." "That really didn't hurt." "You have nothing to be angry about." When in fact the child is feeling great fear, sadness, pain, or anger. We are not talking about the occasional time a parent becomes frustrated with a child and makes such a comment, but a family situation where there is continual discounting of a child's emotions.

   • It is not okay in your family to have needs. Everyone else's needs appear to be more important than yours, and the only way you even get attention is by attending to the needs of others.

   • It is not okay to have successes. Accomplishments are not acknowledged, are many times discounted, or even used as ammunition to shame a child.

▓ *Review the examples* of Emotional Abandonment and circle any you identify with and/or name any that were not noted.

Other acts of abandonment occur when

   • Children cannot live up to the expectations of their parents. These expectations are often unrealistic and not age-appropriate, such as expecting the eight-year-old to remember her dental appointment or the twelve-year-old to be able to manage his younger siblings for hours at a time.

- Holding children responsible for other people's behavior. They may be consistently blamed for the actions and feelings of their parents.
- Showing disapproval toward children that is aimed at their entire being or identity rather than a particular behavior, such as telling a child he is worthless when he does not do his homework, or she is never going to be a good athlete because she missed the final catch of the game. Who the child is isn't separated from what the child does.
- Showing disapproval and rejection for the child due to his or her sexual orientation.

✖ *Circle any of* the above you identify with.

Abandonment and Boundaries

Many times our abandonment issues are fused with distorted, confused, or undefined personal boundaries. We experience abandonment when parents have a distorted sense of boundaries—their boundaries and ours.

> ***When parents do not view us as separate beings with distinct boundaries—we will experience abandonment.***

They want us to like what they like, dress like they dress, and feel as they feel. This is particularly painful during our teenage years when, as part of discovering our own self, we seek out behaviors different from our parents' behaviors. This teenager-parent struggle is common to many. Some parents cannot recognize this as part of the adolescent stage but see it as a personal affront to their image and their own sense of worth. If we in any way express differences from our parents or make different choices than they would, we know we run the risk of rejection.

When parents expect us to be extensions of themselves, fulfilling their dreams—we will feel abandoned.

How many of us went to the school of our father's choosing because he had wanted to attend but had been unable to? How many entered into careers that our parents chose for us? How many of us married who we did or when we did because our parents desired it? I offer a caution in that having done what our parents expected, wanted, or demanded does not mean that it was the wrong thing to do. It just so often means that the decision was never totally ours. It is the *process* that is more painful or possibly wrong, not necessarily the outcome.

Maddy grew up with a brother who had a genetic terminal disease and would die at the age of fourteen. Her mother told both Maddy and her sister that neither of them were to have children due to the possibility of having a child with the same disease who would die early in life. "My mom made it clear that it was not an option for me. Because that decision seemed based in her wanting to protect us from pain and to protect a child from a premature death, it was hard to want to question this dictate. Mom's motivation was sincere. But I was twenty-nine years old when I realized I had never made my own decision about this. Until then it had been my mother's dictate. I realized I had to sit down and separate my life choices from my mother's pain in having a child who died young. I wrestled with the decision for a few years and ultimately made the decision to not have a child. Today, the decision is mine, not my mother's."

Many people do exactly what their parents *don't* want them to do. Often this is a part of their attempt to be a separate person. We don't marry the person our father liked so much. We don't go to the college our mother aspired to attend. We choose to marry the person they would like the least or simply choose to not attend college at all. Again, it is not the outcome that is the issue as much as it is the decision-making process. Instead of choosing freely, we make a reactive decision based in anger.

When parents are not willing to take
responsibility for their feelings, thoughts, and
behaviors, but expect us to take responsibility
for them—we will experience abandonment.

When parents hold children responsible for what should be their responsibility, such as telling the child it is his or her behavior that has caused the breakup of the parents' marriage, or it is the child's behavior that creates the stress that results in the parent's need to drink or use drugs, they are expecting something impossible of a child. In effect, they are telling children that they have more power than they truly have, setting them up to experience futility and inadequacy.

When parents' self-esteem is derived
through our behavior, when their needs
override ours—we feel abandoned.

Henri still feels pain when he talks about how his father publicly gloated over Henri's accomplishments. "Some people told me I should be grateful that my dad even noticed what I was involved in. But there was always something missing about his being proud of me. When I was growing up, I did well in school; I was a very good athlete. I was a student leader and often had my picture in the local paper. My dad came to my events, boasting about me in a way that never seemed real. His boasting was so grand and his need for people to know I was his son was so strong. Yet there was this total lack of interest in me when I was home. When I got home from the ball games, he would already be in bed. He never boasted to me. He never once congratulated me or patted me on the back."

What is important to note is that Henri did not get the validation he needed to feel special, important, or of value to his father. What he believed was that his value to his father was in how he could make his father look to his father's peers.

> *When children are treated as peers with no parent-child distinction—they are abandoned by their parents.*

Many times parents develop relationships with their children in which they are their friends, their peers, their equals. In doing so, they share information that is not age-appropriate for a child. Inappropriate information often creates a sense of burden, or even guilt, for children; that is not fair. To tell a ten-year-old daughter that her father has had an affair cannot offer the daughter any security. The mother may need to talk about it, but that needs to be with someone who has the adult resources to be able to offer appropriate support or feedback. To share with an eight-year-old son the fears related to a situation at work only makes the child feel that his parent is too vulnerable to be available as a source of protection.

> *Abandonment plus distorted boundaries, at a time when children are developing their sense of worth, is the foundation for the belief in their own inadequacy and the central cause of their shame.*

When parents are disrespectful of their children's boundaries and violate them, the message given is that they don't value the child as a person. That message becomes internalized as "I am not of value. I am not worthy." When parents don't acknowledge children's boundaries, the message they give is "You are here to meet my needs," "I am more important than you," and/or "It is not okay to be your own person with individual feelings, desires, or needs." The message also implies that the children have to give up themselves to be available to another. This internalizes to the belief, "I am bad for having different or separate needs, wants, and feelings." "I, in my uniqueness, am not of value." When children experience chronic abandonment with distorted boundaries, they live in fear and doubt about their worth. The greater the clarity a child has around boundaries, understanding who is responsible for what, and the greater a child's self-esteem, the more likely a child will be able to reject, rather than internalize, shameful behaviors and messages.

The following is an example of a young person, Leah, who, in spite of the fact that she was raised in an alcoholic family, experienced some stability in her early years. As a result, she developed a sense of autonomy and self-esteem, which helped her ward off shame. "Up until I was about eight, home seemed okay. I felt valued; life was fun. Then, as if it was overnight, my dad was always angry. My mom was preoccupied and distant or very sad. It was as if neither of our parents had any time for us. Looking back now I realize that something was happening. I just couldn't figure it out. No one was talking about what was wrong. Life just became more and more frightening. I tried to not get in the way. I took care of my brother and sister. I tried to do things to make my dad and mom happy. Nothing I did really made a difference."

One night when she was sixteen and cheerleading at a basketball game, her father showed up so drunk he could hardly walk on his own and created a scene that nearly incited a racial riot. With his arms thrown over her shoulders and her pom-poms tucked under her arms, Leah was leading her drunk father out of the gym when he began to scream racial slurs at a group of African American teenagers. "He said things I never heard him or anyone else say," Leah said. "He said things I never knew he thought. Thank heaven this group of kids couldn't reach us. It was all I could do to get him out of the gym. Everyone was screaming and jeering. Well, I got him into his friend's car and off they went. I didn't know why my dad acted like he did—I was so angry at him."

Leah had the ability to be angry because she had not previously internalized shame and therefore could clearly differentiate who was responsible for what. She had healthy boundary distinction. She knew what took place in the gym was about her father, not her. Because she did not take this incident as a statement about her worth or value, she was also able to access other feelings. With shame we lose the ability to identify our feelings and are more likely to reinstate the Don't Talk rule. Leah said she was angry, and then became sad. She could talk about her fear. While this scene was certainly an act of abandonment by her father, she nonetheless had an emotional boundary that protected her self-worth and her autonomy. Leah's ability to maintain a healthy emotional boundary ("My father's behavior does not determine who I am") prevented her from feeling shamed and personally diminished by her father's behavior.

Corrine was born into an already hectic, frightened family. Her first memories were of hiding behind a table in the kitchen, trying not to be noticed, while listening to her parents arguing and thinking to herself, *Just don't let them see me.* She spent most of her life trying to be invisible. "In my family there was a lot of arguing, unhappiness, and a lot of moving from place to place. I was the youngest of four and an unplanned pregnancy. My mother let me know right away that she was content with three babies, not four. I felt I came out of the chute needing a protective shield, trying to ward off the hurtful words, the painful glares. I was always in their way, yet I worked so hard not to be. My very existence seemed like such a thorn." When childhood is spent on survival, such as Corrine's was, there is little energy left to develop an autonomous or separate sense of self. Corrine was chronically abandoned, subject to emotional boundary abuse; as a result, she experienced and internalized shame.

When we are abandoned by our caretakers we do not perceive that what they did to us was bad; rather, we take the burden of being wrong or bad onto ourselves. We cannot reject them or even their behavior as we so desperately need them. In doing this, we purge the caretakers of being wrong or hurtful, which reinforces a sense of security. In essence, outer safety is purchased at the price of inner security.

> *Abandonment, plus distorted or undefined boundaries as you are developing your worth and identity, creates shame and fear.*

This truth bears repeating because it defines the root of our pain. What we must understand now is that our abandonment experiences and boundary violations were in no way indictments of our innate goodness and value. Instead, they revealed the flawed thinking, false beliefs, and impaired behaviors of those who hurt us. Still, the wounds were struck deep in our young hearts and minds, and the very real pain can still be felt today. The causes of our emotional injury need to be understood and accepted so we can heal. Until we do, the pain will stay with us, becoming a driving force in our adult lives.

■ *Review the summary* boxes in this section of Abandonment and Boundaries and place a check next to those you experienced. Then note the impact that has had on you.

Past-Driven Present Pain

In recovery we seek to change the course in our present lives by healing the pain of our past. As a result of our experiences:

- We adopted false beliefs; that is, "I can't make a mistake or I will be worthless" or "I have to produce to be of value."
- We learned ways to defend against our pain; we may have rationalized, denied, blamed others, etc.
- We developed cognitive defense mechanisms; that is, to deny, minimize, or rationalize. We developed mechanisms to distract us from our pain; that is, excessive behaviors such as overeating, drinking, or drug use. All of these are strategies for the preservation of ourselves when our self is threatened.

Sammy said, "I knew my parents loved me. They provided for me. They came to my school events. They told me they loved me. They would hug me. Yet, they would blatantly reject me if I showed feelings of sadness or anger. There was clearly a Don't Talk rule around being emotional unless the feelings were positive. My shame was for having feelings. So while I knew I was valued in one way, I felt very rejected and abandoned in other ways. There was a lot of loss in my family. My dad lost his job and did not find one for four years. My mother had to be hospitalized for unknown reasons twice when I was between nine and eleven. My sister went to live with my grandmother during those times. And we weren't to talk about any of this. I was angry. I was very frightened. I was sad. I wanted to scream so I could be heard, and yet knew I would not be heard and only banished further."

Sammy did what most of us do when feeling abandonment and fear—she did her best to be lovable so her family would be there for her. Being lovable would be defined by others. For Sammy, it meant discounting her own feelings and needs and putting those of others ahead of hers, which in turn meant disconnecting from her own feelings and needs. Sammy learned these defenses and skills as a young girl; now these are the only defenses and skills she knows for protecting herself and relating to others. Paradoxically, in adulthood, Sammy's beliefs and behaviors no longer protect her, but actually cause her more pain. Unfortunately, this pattern will continue throughout her adult life until the painful weight of chronically discounting her needs and feelings is so great that she is no longer able to continue as she has. Then she will seek new, often harmful protectors, such as alcohol, prescription pills, or food. These present-day defenses will only perpetuate, and probably escalate, her pain until she turns from the course of protection to the path of healing.

Most people develop protective strategies when they are young, carrying them into adulthood, often generalizing the impact into other areas of life. For example, as a child you may have used food to medicate your pain, and continue to use food in this way as an adult, but now you have also added alcohol as a medication. Or, as a child, if you used people-pleasing behaviors to get attention from parents, you may also employ this strategy to get attention in the workplace; it may also fuel an addictive relationship pattern.

The mechanisms we develop to reduce our anxiety and fears are defensive protectors. In no way should we ever be critical of what we needed to do to protect ourselves while growing up. Today, we need to recognize when these defenses and protectors are intrusive in our lives or when they create harm and pain. The purpose or theme of these strategies has been to lessen the pain of abandonment, and also to compartmentalize or distance ourselves from the incredible fear and sense of powerlessness. The basis for all these attempts is to control or compensate for the pain.

The burden of pain we presently carry and try so hard to control is the combination of unresolved pain from the past *plus* pain from the present. As we know, events and family conditions that caused our past pain cannot be changed. Our response to pain is a choice we are making in the present. How we choose to respond can change the course of our lives. In the next few pages, I'll discuss how people respond to pain so you will be able to understand the choices you can make.

Attempts to Control Our Pain

Whether or not we understood the source of our pain in our early lives, we felt it. We were anxious, fearful, saddened, or angry. To live with a high degree of emotional pain was so unbearable for most of us that we sought ways to control the pain to defend against it. Ironically, as we have now seen, those ways of compensating created their own pain. As adults still trying to control our pain, we have sought ways to create a sense of control or power to compensate for the overwhelming experience of powerlessness. We have attempted to control the pain and/or to control the sources of pain. We have tried to be in control to protect ourselves from further exposure so that our vulnerability would not be visible. We have tried to be in control so that no one would ever shame us again and so that we would not have to feel our pain.

We feel our pain. We medicate our pain. We rationalize our pain. These are all responses to the pain we have felt for so long. We first respond to pain on an emotional level, most commonly in terms of victimization, rage, and depression. Then, in an attempt to control the pain, we may respond with behaviors that try to medicate it such as using alcohol, food, and drugs or compulsive behaviors related to sex, money, screens, or relationships. Lastly, we may respond on a rational level, thinking we can avoid the pain if we don't do anything to cause it. Perfectionism and procrastination are two cognitive attempts to control pain by avoiding it.

Emotional Responses to Pain

Victimization as a Response to Pain

Chronic victimization is the result of when we accept and operate on the shameful messages that we internalized as a result of the abandonment. It is a combination of not believing in our own worth and not developing the skills that go with a belief in our worthiness. Setting limits is one such skill. When we have internalized beliefs, such as "I am not worthy," "I am not of value," "Other people are more important than me," or "Other people are more worthy," then it is difficult to set limits. We don't believe we have the right to set limits. We do not know how to say no. Those of us who are victims struggle with appropriate boundaries. We are most apt not to have boundaries or to have boundaries that are easily permeable.

Victims have learned not to trust their own perceptions, believing that another person's perception is more accurate than their own. They always give others the benefit of the doubt and are willing to respond to the structure others set. Victims are not apt to question. In addition to the family rules Don't Talk, Don't Feel, Don't Trust, they have learned the rules Don't Question and Don't Think.

Not believing in their own worth, victims often fail to realize they even have needs and, as a result, do not take care of themselves. They operate from a position of fear, unable to access any anger or indignation that comes with being hurt, disappointed, or even abused. When asked what they need or want, victims often literally do not know.

While the development of the victim response is the result of the belief in personal powerlessness, it is clearly a response to the intense emotional pain in one's life. It not only is an outcome of helplessness, it is also a kind of defense in that victims believe they may not have as much pain if they give in and relinquish their autonomy to someone else.

Victims have developed a high tolerance for pain and for inappropriate behavior. They have become emotionally separated from themselves by becoming highly skilled at rationalizing, minimizing, and often flatly denying the events and emotions in their lives. They are not as readily able to identify others' behavior that has hurt them because that would, in their perception, create a greater feeling of helplessness or invite more trouble. Some victims stay in isolation. Those who choose to stay more visible often play a victim/martyr situation: "Look at how I am victimized. Aren't they terrible for doing this to me! I will just have to endure." Being the victim becomes part of a cycle. Victims already feel bad about themselves as a result of being abandoned and/or used and abused. They don't act in a way that provides safety and security for themselves, leading to greater abandonment or abuse.

Typically, the greater a person's shame, the more likely he or she will invite someone else with shame into their lives. Very often, for the victim, this other person is someone who appears to have the ability to take charge, make things happen, someone who feels strengthened by association with the victim's vulnerability. Depending on the specific history of the two people involved, that attraction often leads to the dominant one battering the victim, either emotionally or physically.

Almost inevitably, victims have great difficulty protecting themselves in the context of intimate relationships. For example, a woman may have such a desperate longing for nurturance and care that it makes it difficult for her to establish safe and appropriate boundaries with others. Her tendency to denigrate herself and to idealize those to whom she becomes attached further clouds her judgment. Typically, her empathic attunement to the wishes of others and her automatic, often unconscious habits of obedience also tend to make her vulnerable to anyone in a position of power or authority. Her defensive style makes it difficult for her to form conscious and accurate assessments of danger.

For all of the reasons noted above, whether male or female, the shameful person is at great risk of repeated victimization.

Rage as Response to Pain

Rage is the holding tank for accumulated fears, angers, humiliations, and shame. It is for many a response of no longer wanting to endure the pain. Emotionally, rage is an attempt to be heard, seen, and valued when people are most desperate and lacking in other resources. For some people rage becomes an integral part of their lifestyle. Growing up, they found anger to be the one safe feeling for them to express, so all their other vulnerabilities were masked with anger. Many people who are rageful don't show any sign of emotions; they keep a tight lid on all of their feelings until something triggers an eruption. There may not be signs of any feeling, and suddenly their rage is in someone else's face. Perhaps it is a scathing memo at work or an outburst of criticism toward a coworker. It could be a lack of tolerance for any disagreement in a discussion, followed by a theatrical exit, or it may take the form of physical or verbal abuse.

People with chronic rage often live isolating lives or live with someone who is the victim of their rage. They tend to move around a lot, wearing out their welcome after relatively short periods of time in one place.

While we may view others' rage as being out of control, those who are ragers feel very much in control and powerful. In their rage they no longer feel inadequate and defective.

Rage is intended to protect against further experiences of pain. Rage is a way of actively compensating for powerlessness and feelings of shame by offering a false sense of power. When rage is the only way people know to protect against their emptiness, powerlessness, and pain, their choice is a quick one. Rageful behavior also offers protection by keeping people at a distance. As a result, other people cannot see into the raging person's inner self that he or she believes to be so ugly.

Rage as a defense also offers protection by transferring the shame to others. The outwardly rageful person chooses a victim-like person who, consciously or not, is willing to take the abuse and take on or assume the shame.

Rage can be accumulated anger that has never seemed safe to expose. When anger is held back, it becomes internalized. With time it grows, festering into chronic bitterness or, even more likely, chronic depression. When there has been no outlet for rage, it is more apt to explode suddenly as a significant single hostile act, such as physical abuse or even murder. Such an act is the consequence of the accumulation of feelings combined with the inability to tolerate painful feelings, to resolve conflict, or to perceive options and choices.

Depression as a Response to Pain

Unfortunately, a depressed person is typically pictured as one who sleeps excessively, is unable to eat, and is suicidal. While that picture represents the severe end of the depression continuum, many depressed adults are able to function daily and meet most of their responsibilities. After all, that has been their survival mode. In my book *It Will Never Happen To Me*, "looking-good" children are described as those raised in a troubled family who maintain the outward appearance of "doing just fine while dying on the inside." They present a false self to the world that may not have the look of depression, but their true self, their emotional and spiritual self, is experiencing great despair. When this is practiced day in and out, week after week, month after month, and year after year, it can easily translate to being "closeted depressed."

To keep depression hidden, those who are depressed avoid getting close enough or spending enough time around others who may recognize their true feelings and the pervasive emptiness their depression is masking. They don't develop close friendships where others are invested enough to pull their covers. They appear very capable and seem to put out an impenetrable force field that says, "Don't ask me about myself. Don't push me." It is difficult enough being depressed. It is even more difficult when there is shame around it—shame as one cause of depression and added shame because they are depressed.

Depression has many causes. It is a biochemical imbalance, a disordered neurochemistry. This could be due to a genetic predisposition. It is commonly accepted among professionals that depression tends to run in families, suggesting there may be a physiological predisposition toward depression. It is also recognized as a consequence of a habitually pessimistic and disordered way of viewing the world. It can be a consequence of loss and the inability to do the grief work necessary to bring completion to the feelings of sorrow. But for many, their depression is a consequence of trauma.

There is tremendous loss associated with being raised in a shame-based family. With the family being denial-centered, as it often is, and it not being okay to talk honestly, the sense of loss is amplified because there is no way to work through the pain. The hurt, the disappointment, the fears, and the anger associated with life events, as well as with abandonment experiences, are all swirled together and internalized. When you add to this a personal belief that says you are at fault, it is easy to see why you came to believe in your unworthiness, and so try to hide your real self from others. Eventually, whether you are thirty-five or fifty-five, you suddenly hit a wall. The burden of hiding becomes too heavy and all of those protecting, controlling mechanisms that kept you going for so long just stop working. The depression becomes obvious.

Most people who experience depression related to loss are extremely frightened of their feelings. And they have so much to feel about. When it is not safe to speak these feelings, they become directed inward against the self. This becomes another means of perpetuating shame, which then further protracts the depressive mood.

As discussed in Chapter One, there are necessary and unnecessary losses in life. Because it was not safe to acknowledge them, you didn't learn coping skills for the losses that would occur in your adult years. So, when a loss occurs and/or accumulates in adulthood, you resort to the same defenses you learned in childhood to deny what you are feeling.

When we have had chronic loss and traumatic stress in our lives, many of us develop thought processes wherein we catastrophize and exaggerate fear to such a point that we feel hopeless and in despair. For example, when your husband is twenty minutes late for an important appointment, you think he must have been in a terrible car accident. When your boss forgot to say hello, you feel certain that she is angry with you and is going to fire you. Armed with some small bit of knowledge, we presume the worst will happen.

Over the years, given our experiences, we have developed a committee of internal voices that have become our Inner Critic, telling ourselves we are stupid, not wanted, ugly, and unimportant; this is in response to any slight or perceived loss, or when we feel slighted by someone we value.

Most adults from troubled families experience a combination of both unresolved loss, trauma, and a pessimistic view of life. When we feel our powerlessness, our despair, and our fear, we send ourselves into a downhill spiral so quickly that anybody's head would be spinning.

Acute Episodes of Depression

Many adults make their way through life cut off from their internal pain, until they experience a significant present-day loss—the last child leaving home, a significant health problem, the death of a close friend or family member, infidelity of a partner, the loss of job or career opportunity. As great numbers of women enter perimenopausal and menopausal stages, the combination of physical changes and the symbolism around such changes can create an incredible sense of loss. For men and women both, one significant present-day loss can be the straw that breaks the camel's back. In other words, the new loss can trigger the beginning of a downward emotional spiral in which the adult becomes overwhelmed in despair, shame, powerlessness, and depression. Carmella, who was raised in a physically abusive family, was a department manager in an engineering firm. She had tucked away the pain of her childhood history into a corner of her heart and put a lock on it. She was involved in raising her own family and kept a distant relationship with her sister and parents. All aspects of her life were compartmentalized. Then one day, she lost her oldest daughter in an accident. Six months after that, her father died. Three weeks later, Carmella made her first suicide attempt. To lose a child is one of life's greatest tragedies for anyone. Further, Carmella had no skills, no internal supports to deal with the intense pain when her daughter died. While she did not feel close to her father, his death unleashed all of the childhood pain she had so neatly and quietly tucked away. When present-day loss occurs, we may not be aware of remembering our growing-up years, but we are certainly feeling the accumulated pain.

Tom, who was raised in an extremely critical home and felt his loss through chronic rejection, quickly separated from his parents and all his siblings after high school. Then, at the age of twenty-eight when his fiancée broke up with him, his exaggerated and catastrophic thinking led into incredible despair. He had talked himself into seeing himself as totally unworthy. He envisioned that his fiancée would marry someone much more financially stable than he was and certainly a lot more fun and exciting. She would have children with someone else. He would be alone all of his life. He was convinced he would never find happiness, and he would never be able to offer anything to anyone else. On and on and on, Tom's self-defeating painful thinking continued. Soon, he was sleeping twelve to fourteen hours a day, missing days at work, and no longer exercising or eating properly.

Losing a relationship, particularly in young adulthood, happens to many of us. However, because of chronic losses in his childhood, Tom had not learned the skills needed to grieve through the loss of his fiancée. He was not able to understand the experience in any way except as further evidence of his inadequacy and worthlessness. This loss was simply one more that added fuel to his already existing fire of shame.

Like victimization, depression is a consequence of the inability to defend and protect ourselves against the pain of loss.

Suicide: The Most Severe Response to Pain

"I am hopeless. I am unworthy, and I don't deserve to live. Life won't get any better, and I can't stand this pain." Suicidal thoughts, attempts, and completions speak of many issues. They are often a reflection of anger, rage turned inward, and depression. For some people, the act of suicide seems to grant power that compensates for the powerlessness in their life. For others, death is perceived to be a better option than living with certain memories and shame. The pain is too overwhelming and, out of despair and hopelessness, people become their own victims. Thoughts of taking one's own life are much more prevalent than people realize. While pain creates such thoughts, these individuals also experience shame for having the thoughts. My message to you is this: *Please don't feel ashamed. But, please do speak up and let someone know how frightened, angry, or hopeless you are feeling.*

In recovery, you can speak about those issues that have created the pain. You can say no to your shame. You can learn ways to express your anger without hurting yourself. You can develop new beliefs and behaviors that support you in the way you deserve to be supported. You can learn how to access the power within you that does exist. You deserve to be able to live without pain. But when you are considering suicide as a way out of your pain, you must reach out and get assistance from a helping professional.

> ✖ *If you identify* with the emotional responses of victimization, rage, depression, or suicidal ideation or attempts, describe the impact that has had on your life.

Behavioral Responses to Pain

"Medicating" Pain

Whether your emotional response to pain is one of victimization, rage, or depression, you may also try different behaviors to control your pain, hoping to lessen the hurt. Unfortunately, your efforts to control the pain do not remove the cause or source of your feelings. One way people try to control and regulate their pain is by "medicating" it through addiction to substances or compulsive behaviors.

Substance Use Disorders

Types of substance use disorders (addictions) may include dependency on food, caffeine, nicotine, sugar, alcohol and/or other drugs. Many of the substances people become addicted to are socially sanctioned and supported, making it very difficult for those who abuse these substances to see how they are using them in unhealthy ways.

In addition to temporarily controlling your pain, the substances you use and abuse often provide something you did not know how to seek naturally. As an example, alcohol may give a sense of power to someone who has only known powerlessness. It may give access to a sense of courage and confidence to someone who feels lacking. This is certainly drug-induced, temporary, and false, but for many people, false is better than none. For someone who is isolated and feels alienated from others, alcohol makes it easier to reach out to people. "Give me a little bit to drink and I become alive. I pull myself away from the wall and I find myself talking, laughing, listening. I see people responding to me and I like it." This kind of thinking doesn't mean that a person is addicted, but it does mean he or she is thirsty for connection with others. In this case, alcohol becomes the reinforcement in order to feel whole and complete.

For people who have never taken time for play or laughter because life has been so serious and "I have to get things done," alcohol gives them the opportunity to relax. Alice identified, "My entire life has been spent taking care of other people. I am always busy. I make these lists daily, thinking the world will stop if I don't get the job done. I don't think about missing out on fun—it has never been a part of my life.

"I was a teetotaler. I never drank until I was twenty-six. I don't even know why I started. But those first few times I remember thinking that I was being silly, hearing myself laugh with other people. It actually scared me. Yet at the same time there was this attraction. It was as if there was this whole other part of me I didn't know and maybe was okay to know.

"The attraction to relaxing with alcohol kept getting stronger. I can actually remember thinking, *I don't have to make this decision tonight*, or *I don't have to do this by myself*. Pretty soon it was, *I don't have to do this at all*. I was having fun. I was relaxing." Alice's new ways of letting go and becoming less rigid were not harmful, but because she did not know how to relax without alcohol she ultimately became dependent on it. Alice, like so many others, was seeking wholeness. But the only glimpse she had of it was "under the influence."

Variations of this scenario fit for other addictions. Our relationship to certain foods or the intake, lack of intake, and/or purging of food may be about an internal struggle with power and control. We may be attempting to access power that we don't have the skills or confidence to access more naturally. Starving ourselves, purging, and compulsive overeating may be anger turned toward ourselves. Possibly we are punishing ourselves for being bad. The anorexic may be literally starving herself to become invisible in response to shame; the anorexic and bulimic may be seeking perfection—which is based in shame.

When we come from a pain-based family, it is common to go outside of ourselves for a quick answer to relieve our suffering. It doesn't seem possible that we have any way to help ourselves. Yet, ultimately, we can keep our pain under control only so long before it starts to leak out. Frightened, we feel out of control and we seek a medicator. Sometimes that medicator is a person or possibly an activity; many times it is a substance. Often it is a combination of compulsions and addictions.

Process/Behavioral Addictions

To experience shame and powerlessness is to be in unbearable pain. While physical pain is horrible, there are moments of relief. There is hope of being cured. However, when we believe we are defective, there is no cure. Shame is a defeated state. We have no relationship with ourselves or anyone else; we are totally alone. Relief from this intolerable pain must come, one way or another. We need someone or something to take away our profound loneliness and fear, and so we seek a mood-altering experience. We need an escape. Everyone has certain behaviors used as a way to escape, but it is when we come to depend on them to relieve our unworthiness that these become compulsive in nature. And when we grow up in an environment of shaming, where the cause of pain is external, we develop the belief that the solutions to problems exist only externally through substances or behaviors that are medicators. Addiction is not as much about a specific substance or activity as it is about disrupting the normal procession of pleasure and process of thinking. Both substances and process addictions stimulate and reward the same neural pathways in the brain. The part of the brain that allows you to think rationally and see choices and consequences becomes hijacked when under the influence, leaving the brain to not consider consequences.

There are many different types of addiction ranging from compulsively repeated activities to preoccupying thoughts to relationship dependencies. We may use some form of keeping busy to distance or to distract ourselves, to get our minds off our pain, our fear, or our anger. We keep busy to stay in control of our feelings and therefore to avoid feeling bad. Many behavioral compulsions would be otherwise harmless activities if they weren't exaggerated, destroying the balance in our lives. For example, exercise is a healthy activity until done so excessively that we actually injure our bodies.

Relationship addiction is the dependence on being in a relationship to validate our worth. That means we use other people to lessen our shame and to avoid truly facing our selves.

Sex addiction is the use of sexual stimulation to act as a detractor or medicator of pain; or it may be a false way of accessing power to overcome our sense of powerlessness. Compulsive sex experiences can temporarily offer us warmth and an appearance of love. Or we can act out sex as an expression of anger. These sex experiences may temporarily affirm that we are lovable and worthy, all the while compounding our belief in our defectiveness. Sex addicts vary in their focus, from obsessive masturbating, the use of pornographic materials, exhibitionism, obscene phone calls, voyeurism, to multiple affairs, use of prostitutes, and so on. For sex addicts, certain behaviors take on sexual meaning. They view objects and people through their sexual preoccupation.

Even though compulsive behaviors distract and alter feelings, feelings themselves can become compulsive in nature. We become dependent on certain feelings to mask and avoid experiencing what we are really feeling. We may become addicted to rage, using it as a release for all feelings. Fear can overwhelm us, where phobias, hypervigilance, and anxieties can control our lives.

While some compulsions are certainly more harmful to ourselves and our family, others may be considered only nuisances. Substances and behaviors can detract from our pain and, therefore, represent attempts to control whether or not we feel such pain. Yet any time we use a substance or become involved in a process or behavior that interferes with our honesty, our ability to be present with ourselves, it deserves our attention.

    ❖ *If you identify* with the behavioral response to pain and/or substance or process addictions, describe the impact it has had on your life.

Cognitive Responses to Pain

While some people focus on controlling the pain itself, others attempt to control the source of the pain. *Control* is the key word here. These people hope to control the cause of the pain, as opposed to removing, releasing, or healing it. As with the emotional and behavioral responses discussed earlier, these cognitive or rational responses try to prevent potential abandonment and prevent the possibility of exposing a shameful self.

Perfectionism

A common rational or cognitive response to pain is perfectionism. Perfectionism is driven by the belief that if a person's behavior is perfect, there will be no reason to be criticized and therefore no more cause for pain. However, perfectionism is a shame-based phenomenon because children learn that "no matter what they do, it's never good enough." As a result, in their struggle to feel good about themselves and relieve the source of pain, they constantly push to excel, to be the best.

Highly perfectionistic people are usually people who have been raised in a rigid family environment. The rigidity may be in the form of unrealistic expectations that parents have for their children and/or for themselves. In these situations, the children internalize the parents' expectations. Also, rigidity may be expressed as children feel the need to do things "right" in order to gain approval from their parent and to lessen fears of rejection. For most children, being "right" is perceived to mean there is no room for mistakes.

Let's look at the example of Teri, nineteen years old, in a therapy group and talking about being a perfectionist. "When I was in junior high school, in order to be able to visit with friends on Saturday afternoon I had to complete certain household tasks. So, every Saturday morning I would approach my father to get a list of what I needed to accomplish to be able to go out later in the day. I'd pick up his list and go on about my duties. When the list was completed, I'd return it to my father, but then he would give me a second list. When I was done with that list, I was inevitably given a third list. Many times there was a fourth and fifth list."

As you can guess, Teri didn't spend a lot of Saturday afternoons with her friends. When Teri told this story, tears streamed down her cheeks. Then she paused and reflectively commented, "But we all come from some pretty crazy families. It could have been worse. Besides, I learned a few things. If you want something done, ask me. I know how to be quick." Then, haltingly she added, "What I really learned, though, was that no matter what I do, it's never good enough."

That was the lesson for Teri. No matter what she did, it wasn't good enough. Nothing was good enough because it wasn't humanly possible to please her father. That Saturday ritual was not about Teri. It was about her father and his need to control, his need for power. Whether or not Teri was permitted to spend time with her friends was not about how well or how quick she was in her work. For her own well-being, Teri would need to acknowledge that. In doing so, she would be able to establish an emotional boundary, separating her worth from her father's severe criticism. She would be saying no to the shame she had internalized that told her she wasn't good enough. She could then start to counter the shame-based message by acknowledging her worth.

Unfortunately, most perfectionists have no internal sense of limits. With shame and fear nipping at their heels the entire time, they always perceive their performance as related to a standard or judgment outside themselves. As children, they were taught to strive onward. There was never a time or place to rest or to have inner joy and satisfaction.

Perfection as a performance criteria means you never measure up. Then, not measuring up is translated into a comparison with others of good versus bad, better versus worse. Inevitably, you end up feeling the lesser for the comparison. Comparison with others is one of the primary ways people continue to create more shame for themselves. You continue to do to yourself on the inside what was done to you from the outside. Since your efforts were never experienced as sufficient, adequate, or good enough, you did not develop an internal sense of how much is good enough.

As adults, we need to identify those areas where we once strived so hard for recognition, attention, and approval. Then we need to come to the understanding that not only did we do our best, but we truly were good enough. The lack of acceptance we have felt is not about us or our worth, but a residue left from those who judged us and who sought power by threatening to reject us. While we were not able to understand that as children, we can come to terms with that as adults today.

Procrastination

Procrastination, such as starting but not completing a project or considering a project but never initiating it, is often an attempt to defend against further shame. Perfectionism and procrastination are closely linked. It is easy to picture Teri, in the example given, never finishing her first list, realizing that she could not please her father. Teri, though, believed in herself a bit more strongly than most people who procrastinate. Often, the procrastinator has little confidence and more fear. The perfectionist is more apt to follow through because there is the possibility of the reinforcement of some sense of accomplishment. The procrastinator will not even see that possibility.

Some children received so little attention that they were not encouraged to initiate projects, let alone complete them. Too many times when these children did something, drew a picture or wrote a story and gleefully showed their parents, the parents barely looked at it and then set it aside or maybe even lost it. When there is no positive reinforcement to complete school projects or homework, children perform with ambivalence. They believe that "No one else cares" and develop the attitude, "Why should I care?" The result is procrastination and ambivalence.

It was just as painful for children when their parents did pay attention but were constantly critical, maybe making a joke of the children's work, possibly humiliating them in front of others. Stacey, who was an average student in school, became very excited about a history project during her sophomore year of high school. "I worked hard on it all quarter, which was unusual for me, but I found this real interesting and the teacher liked me.

For the first time in a long time I really wanted to do something well. One night I was at the dining room table putting all of the pages of my report in a notebook to be turned in the next day in class. I wasn't expecting my parents to come home for a few hours yet, so I was shocked when my mother and stepfather came in, both laughing loudly, both drunk. Mom asked what I was doing and then picked up my paper which was titled, 'Did America Need To Be In World War II?' Suddenly, she was in a rage and calling me a communist, saying I wasn't patriotic.

"It was unreal. Within minutes, they were both screaming at me, calling me all kinds of names. They took my report and, in their words, threw the 'trash' into the fireplace. Well, there was no way I could tell the teacher what had happened. I just took a failing grade. It was pretty horrifying, but I should have known not to put that much effort into anything. Most things never worked out for me too much."

Stacey's sense of defeat was a culmination of similar experiences. Whenever she put forth effort to achieve, she felt diminished. It was several years before she could put into perspective the report incident and all the smaller incidents that led her to believe that even if she wanted to work at something, it probably wasn't worth the effort. As a result, Stacey quit trying to achieve at a very young age.

When children are humiliated for their efforts, made to feel inadequate or stupid, they find ways to protect themselves so they cease involvement in any action that would prove they really are a failure.

In addition, children become discouraged when they are constantly compared to someone who did it better or might have done it better. Tom says he was always compared to his two older brothers. "My two older brothers were articulate. They were quick and did well in school. It took me longer to grasp things. I wasn't as interested in math and sciences as they were. I was more interested in my friends. So, with school being more of a struggle and having no real help from my parents, only the push that 'you should be like your brothers,' I just gave up. I wasn't like them and didn't want to be."

Also mixed into procrastination can be anger, expressed as an attitude of "I'll show you—I won't finish this," or "I'll only do it part way. I won't give my best." Inherent in this attitude is a challenge that insists, "Like me for who I am, not for what I do." In a family where rigidity is the rule, where it is not okay to make mistakes, not okay to take risks or be different, not okay to draw attention to yourself, you learn not to initiate or not to finish what you started. For those of us raised this way, it is amazing that we get anything done.

❧ *If you identify* with the Cognitive Responses to Pain of perfectionism and/or procrastination, describe how they have impacted your life.

Understanding Your Defenses Against Pain

Rage, depression, victimization, addictions, compulsions, perfectionism, and procrastination—these are some of the responses to having lived with fear and pain. Such responses often become protectors. They offer ways to control the pain itself and/or control the source of the pain. Other protectors begin as common, everyday acts, but taken to extremes create negative outcomes in the long run. Some of these are intellectualization, physical isolation, humor, magical thinking, lying, silence, and withdrawal.

❧ *Make a list* of defenses you developed to defend against the pain. Are those still behaviors you use today? After you make your list, then ask yourself the following questions:

- What did it [the protective behavior] do for you in the past?
- What is it doing for you now?
- Would you like to let go of it?
- What do you need to do to let it go?
- What is interfering with your ability to let go of it?

Our pain, our choice of responses, and the consequences of our choices are summarized on the chart, "From a Past of Chronic Loss to the Turning Point: The Experience of Pain from an Adult's Point of View."

From a Past of Chronic Loss to the Turning Point
The Experience of Pain from an Adult's Point of View

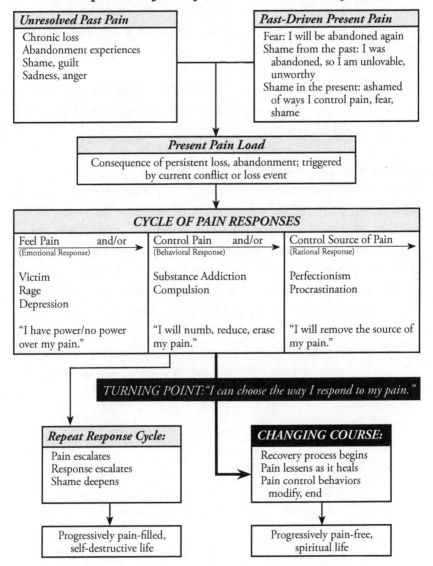

Unresolved Past Pain	*Past-Driven Present Pain*
Chronic loss Abandonment experiences Shame, guilt Sadness, anger	Fear: I will be abandoned again Shame from the past: I was abandoned, so I am unlovable, unworthy Shame in the present: ashamed of ways I control pain, fear, shame

Present Pain Load

Consequence of persistent loss, abandonment; triggered
by current conflict or loss event

CYCLE OF PAIN RESPONSES

Feel Pain and/or (Emotional Response)	Control Pain and/or (Behavioral Response)	Control Source of Pain (Rational Response)
Victim Rage Depression	Substance Addiction Compulsion	Perfectionism Procrastination
"I have power/no power over my pain."	"I will numb, reduce, erase my pain."	"I will remove the source of my pain."

TURNING POINT: *"I can choose the way I respond to my pain."*

Repeat Response Cycle:	CHANGING COURSE:
Pain escalates Response escalates Shame deepens	Recovery process begins Pain lessens as it heals Pain control behaviors modify, end

Progressively pain-filled, self-destructive life	Progressively pain-free, spiritual life

Causes of past pain cannot be changed.
Responses to pain, both past and present, can change.
Changing responses to pain changes the course of pain in life.

Letting Go of the Past, Healing the Pain

Every one of us would like to rid ourselves of pain. The answer lies in being willing to acknowledge your pain. That means facing the feelings. It means being willing to own the sadness, the hurt and fears, the embarrassments and anger about how you had to live your life. It means being willing to be specific about all the ways you fought for emotional survivorship, how you attempted to compensate for powerlessness, and how you tried to gain control to overcome the incredible sense of shame and fear that has been so significant in your life.

> ✚ *Ultimately, you will* need to identify the loss events, conditions, and shaming messages in your adult life, as well as those in your growing-up years, in order to be able to become separate from them. An adult loss graph, like the loss graph of your early years, is a very useful way to begin to identify the difference between who you are and what has happened to you. See Appendix C for a Loss Graph form with instructions on how to record the losses in your adult years.

We Can't Go Forward without Finishing the Past

To go forward, we must finish and let go of the past. Jill Johnston, author of *Mother Bound,* writes that as we let go of the past "we alter the way we see ourselves in the present and the way we cast ourselves into the future. . . . The notion of who has rights, whose voice can be heard, whose individuality is worthy, comes under revision and the shame of difference will evaporate."

To let go of our pain, we must also acknowledge what we have been doing in the present to control our pain. Facing our own painful reality, both past and present, empowers us by giving us choice.

One option is that we can remain role players, acting out old family roles, directed by negative judgments and false beliefs about ourselves. Choosing this option, of course, we are not really attempting to finish the past. Also, we are consigning ourselves to a future weighted down by the need to manage our shame and pain.

The other option we have is to become free agents, choosing to set our own course and act according to our own freely chosen beliefs, rather than the dictates of external standards. On this course we are able to finish the past because we are no longer being controlled by it.

Finishing the past does not mean that it disappears from our memories. Instead, it simply takes its rightful place as one significant dimension of our personal history.

Letting go of our pain doesn't mean that we will, or should, forget our suffering. That would be another kind of denial. In time we can learn to honor our past pain much as we would honor a soldier returning from war. We can also honor our experience as a significant part of our life's struggle to grow and survive.

Freeing ourselves from pain is what recovery is all about. Releasing ourselves from the past and freeing ourselves from the painful limitations of our past-driven present life is the process we go through as we turn to the new reality we want. Remember that recovery takes time. But it can be done. It can happen to you, to me, to all of us.

The awareness we now have brings us to another turning point to recovery:

> ↳ The pain we feel is not only from the past, but also from the past-driven present.

> ↳ We were powerless in the past, but we are not powerless in the present.

Another turning point comes with another awareness:

> ↳ We are not our pain.

We are much, much more than mere embodiments of pain. Realizing that truth allows us to separate ourselves from our emotional responses. Further, our own response is something we can affect, something we can make a choice about. As Steven Covey writes, "Responsibility is response-ability."

Together, these awarenesses lead us to the turning point that can put us on the path of freedom:

↳ Our pain is our responsibility.

↳ What we do about our pain is a choice we make.

Chapter Three

Steps to Freedom

The Process of Recovery from Chronic Loss

"It is true that as long as we live we may keep repeating the patterns established in childhood. It is true that the present is powerfully shaped by the past. But it is also true that . . . insight at any age keeps us from singing the same sad songs again."
—Judith Viorst

"It is not possible to be honest in the here and now when you continue to discount and minimize your childhood experiences."
—Claudia Black

For adults from troubled families who turn to a new course for their lives, the process of recovery brings renewed energy, new understandings, and new hope.

- Recovery is actively taking responsibility for how you live your life today.
- Recovery is being able to put the past behind. It's no longer having your childhood script dominate how you live your life today.
- Recovery is being able to speak the truth about your growing-up years.

- Recovery is the process in which you develop skills you weren't able to learn in your childhood.
- Recovery is a process, not an event, often beginning as a result of a professionally directed treatment or therapy or experiences in self-help groups.
- Recovery is no longer living a life based in fear or shame.
- Recovery is developing your sense of self separate from survival/coping mechanisms. Your identity is no longer based in reaction, but action.
- Recovery is the process of identifying, owning, and developing healthy ways of expressing feelings; it is the process of learning self-love, self-acceptance. From learning these new ways, a person often learns how to set healthy boundaries and limits, to get needs met, to play, relax, and develop flexibility.
- Recovery is the process of learning to trust yourself and then trusting others, and with trust comes the opportunity for intimacy.

A person is truly on a recovery course when new belief systems and new behaviors are actualized in relationships at work, with friends and family, in the most intimate love and sexual relationships, and in taking care of oneself physically and emotionally.

People reach their turning points in different ways. Some begin in twelve-step programs, others through their religious beliefs, through spiritual healing, and/or professional therapy services. Whatever brings you to your new beginning, you will need to attend to some core issues from your past, so that they no longer dictate how you live your life today.

In Chapter Two, we looked at the general causes and the dynamics of past pain: chronic loss, abandonment, fear, and shame. You will need to identify the specific events and conditions in your own life, those that were played out in your past, and those that continue to cause pain in the present. To resolve your feelings and revise your beliefs and relearn behaviors, you will need to incorporate four identified, important steps that are the backbone of the recovery process. Each time you face a particular issue, you will need to go through all four of these steps.

Four Steps to Recovery

   Step One: Explore past losses.
   Step Two: Connect the past to present life.
   Step Three: Challenge internalized beliefs.
   Step Four: Learn new skills.

The steps to recovery, along with the feelings, processes, and skills needed, are illustrated on the chart, "Changing Course: The Recovery Process."

Step One: Explore Past Losses

"What Happened That Hurt Me?"
"What Didn't I Have That I Needed?"

Much of the initial part of the recovery process involves talking about the past. Many people find this both exciting and scary, but some wonder why it is necessary. As I mentioned earlier, if recalling something from the past feels like you have to drag it up, there is almost always unresolved pain attached to the experience that still affects you today. Clearly, the purpose of talking about the past is to put it behind us.

   To let go of the past you must be willing to break through your denial so you can grieve your pain. In other words, you have to admit to yourself the truth of what happened, rather than hide or keep secret the hurt and wounds that occurred. Admitting the truth is not meant to be a process of blaming our parents. In fact, as we go back and explore the past, we may not even choose to share the information with our parents. Whether or not you do is a very individual matter.

   One does not explore the past to assign blame but to discover and acknowledge reality. Very often adults still operate on beliefs formed in childhood. Looking back at specific past events may cause a major shift in perspective. For instance, if our parents had hit us in anger, our childhood assumption was that they were angry at us for something we did wrong or that we were inadequate in some way. As adults we can see that our parents were really angry with themselves, or angry about something else in their lives, a job loss, for example. As vulnerable children we were easy targets, so we were the ones who were hit but for entirely different reasons than we believed.

Our newly acquired understanding is a critical step in the process of creating positive beliefs about ourselves. However, acknowledging the reality, in this case that our parents hit us, is also essential. We can no longer afford to be held hostage by this shameful secret. Acknowledging the reality of what happened allows us to feel and grieve the pain.

Exploring the past is very important because it may be the first time in our lives that we have been able to talk openly about our experiences. As we complete our loss graphs we will be able to identify those specific events and conditions that caused pain and restricted our lives. Talking without the fear of being rejected or punished allows us to release deep feelings that we have kept inside and that remain hurtful to us. When we do this with other people participating in the same process, we receive validation for who we were when we were young. The word validate comes from the Latin *valere*, "to make strong." Being validated makes us strong.

Most of us who grew up with chronic loss need to talk with others about our experiences to help us recognize our needs and to learn how to set appropriate limits and boundaries. We will be able to discard the messages that we aren't good enough or that we are inadequate. Then we begin to understand that we are of real value. This should not be an isolated process. Sharing our painful experiences with others who understand creates a needed support system.

A major purpose in going back and talking about the past is to break the denial process and start speaking the truth. It's difficult when you've had to deny, minimize, or discount the first fifteen or twenty years of your life. While denial became a skill that served you as a child in a survival mode, its continued use today interferes in adult experiences. When you have worked through this process you can begin to learn to be honest about what is occurring in the present, in the here and now.

As an adult, it is easy to continue to minimize, discount, rationalize, but these are behaviors that block the honest identification and expression of feelings. They impede your ability to be honest with yourself and others. This greatly impacts self-esteem and interpersonal relationships. Owning your experiences in childhood greatly relieves the burden of defending yourself as an adult and gives you a beginning of choice. Exploring the past is an act of empowerment.

The Process for Healing Feelings from the Past

As we discover and acknowledge painful realities in our past we are, at the same time, doing our grief work. We are identifying and grieving the losses that occurred in our lives. Because the pain of these losses has not been acknowledged or validated, taking the time to grieve for ourselves is important. Left unexamined and without appropriate avenues for expression, these feelings of loss can grow into emotional time bombs We act them out in depression, addictions, compulsive behaviors, hurtful relationships, difficulties with parenting, and so on. It is common to hear people say, "I feel as if something is missing." That something missing is often what we needed, but didn't get.

Grief encompasses a series of universal emotional reactions. It always begins with loss and from that loss comes shock. We are numb to what has occurred; some people vacillate between disbelief and acknowledging the reality. Many of us move into denial, as the loss is too painful to acknowledge. Sadness, anger, guilt are normal feelings that people often cycle through several times. Some people engage in bargaining, often between themselves and their God or Higher Power. Ultimately, we most likely find a way to accept the reality of the new norm and move forward.

While adults from troubled families are not grieving death per se, they are grieving losses often chronic in nature. When loss is chronic and there is a likelihood of abandonment at emotionally painful times, we would be more apt to bypass the shock stage of grief and quickly move into denial. Often we become so skilled at this we have difficulty even identifying a situation to be a loss. "No, it wasn't important to me that my father didn't come home at night. He would have been drunk anyway." "No, it didn't bother me that my mom slapped me. I was used to it. It didn't really hurt."

Anger is a natural response to loss. It is a protest, which is an attempt to retrieve that which is gone. But, unfortunately, when people are frightened of rejection, distrusting of their own perceptions, and greatly dependent on others' approval, they have difficulty owning their anger. They don't want to be angry. They want to be understanding. As a result, many people find it easier to move to guilt or sadness. The inability to identify anger interferes with the ability to move through the grief process.

The natural sorrow that is a part of the grief process is where many people become stuck. When we face losses with an internal belief that we aren't worthy, we are more likely to succumb to the power of depression and experience a more chronic state of depression.

Both true and false guilt is a natural response to a loss. True guilt is a feeling of regret or remorse over something we have done. False guilt is a feeling of regret or remorse for someone else's behavior and actions, such as believing I am responsible for my mother's depression or my father's absence. Because we have greater difficulty delineating true from false guilt, we are more apt to become stuck in this stage of the grief process. As a result, we continue to wonder what it was that *we* could have done to have made things different. "If I had only gone to sleep like I was supposed to . . ." or "If I had been a good enough kid." The false guilt we carry with us also keeps us stuck in the bargaining stage.

As painful as it is for anyone to wend their way through a grief process, many people find a type of psychological safety in their bargaining. To let go of the bargaining and to reach a healthy place of acceptance you have to allow yourself to acknowledge and tolerate the intensity of your feelings. Acceptance comes as a result of being able to experience each step of this grief process. When it isn't safe to feel, we cannot get to that acceptance.

> ⚏ *As you review* your process with grief, describe where you are more apt to get stuck. Is it with the guilt, the anger, the denial, or the sadness? What are the beliefs that keep you stuck? These are often beliefs such as "It's not okay to be angry?" "Suck it up, you are weak if you have these feelings." What self-care behavior can you practice while you are exploring your losses? Self-care includes behaviors such as eating healthy, getting adequate sleep or exercise, talking to others, and asking for help.

By knowing more about grief and your own history, you are more armed to meet your past or present-day losses. It is necessary to continue with Step One of Exploring Past Losses:

1. Identify the losses (the wrongs, the hurts) that happened as a child. Not only is it important to grieve the wrongs and hurts, but it is of value to mourn the loss of what you didn't have.
2. Allow yourself to feel your losses. It is important that you feel, in addition to identifying and understanding what happened.
3. Share those feelings with others. Sharing feelings is a way of bringing light and air to the wound, allowing it to heal. Shame subsides when a wound is no longer secret; it disappears in the light of another's acceptance.

There is no specific timetable in which one moves through their grief. If you address past losses with the aid of a therapist, grief workshop, or books, the process moves more quickly. For most people, it is a process they periodically come back to as specific issues come up.

A Cognitive Life Raft and Emotional Safety Net

Before people are ready to feel the feelings associated with the past, they need to have an intellectual understanding of how past events have affected them. They need to have information about what is normal; that is, how their environments differed from other environments that did not result in a restricted life of lasting pain. They need to hear others talk about experiences similar to their own. Reading about others' similar experiences also helps so they will have a language to understand and talk about their own experiences.

Gaining these insights and understandings allows you to know you are not crazy. You are not bad. There are reasons for your feelings. This process provides a sense of safety and a cognitive life raft.

You will also need an emotional safety net. This occurs when you form a trusting relationship with the person(s) who will guide you through your process. In order to walk back through the pain, there must be a feeling of trust of self and the trust of at least one significant other with whom you will work through the process. While you need to own your fears, sadness, hurt, and anger, you don't necessarily want to do that with your parents; however, you will want to do it with a counselor, other recovering adults, or a trusted friend.

We need to feel safe in order to trust and to share our vulnerabilities. That will take time. For some, it is easier to experience their grief than to develop an emotional safety net. In our childhood, when we trusted someone vital to our emotional well-being, we were often betrayed. Consequently, our fear of trusting means that we will need time to struggle with our feelings when we begin to trust significant others again. It is this process that eventually leads us to the acceptance and validation of the children we once were.

Compared to the other steps in the recovery process, the first step of exploring and grieving the past is the most emotionally painful part of recovery. At times, recovering adults have been criticized for focusing on the past too much or for staying in the problem, as opposed to searching for a solution. However, at this point, we are in the process of owning our childhood experiences (grieving losses) and we must take whatever time we need. Everything can't be remembered at the same time, nor do feelings come to the surface all at once.

Grounding Practices

We also need to develop an internal emotional safety net, and that can be developed with the ongoing process of what is called *grounding practices*. Grounding practices help you to stay emotionally regulated and to not move into a trauma response of flight, fight, or freeze. Doing this work can tap a depth of feelings you have worked hard to avoid and may bring up feelings that you have little experience tolerating. Grounding practices are meant to be used throughout recovery and healing and not just at times of vulnerability. The skills you incorporate by doing them are like having a savings account that is there for you as a backup to draw upon. The good news it they are readily available, and you may find you have naturally gravitated toward them. They may account for some of the resiliency you are already demonstrating.

Some common forms of grounding include:

- Playing music
- Listening to music
- Singing
- Dancing
- Crafts such as beadwork, needlepoint, woodwork
- Arts such as pottery, photography, painting, sculpting
- Nature walks
- Time with animals
- Gardening
- Engagement with martial arts
- Meditation practices

Ideally these are regular practices you integrate into your life. They can calm racing thoughts, lessen depression, reduce anxiety, increase compassion for yourself and others. They can be fun and offer meaning in your life.

> ■ *What grounding practices* do you already engage in? Consider whether or not it's feasible to increase the frequency or regularity in which you engage them. What new grounding practices are you willing to investigate?

Fear of Feelings

Fear of feelings makes it difficult for most of us to talk about the past. Where there is loss, there will be tears. Where there is loss, there will be anger. We must be willing to show our feelings. Feelings don't go away. Repressed feelings only serve to distract us from our real self. We must speak to the sadness, the anger, the fears that we never had an opportunity to own or express and grieve for how we had to live our lives.

You probably have a lot of fear about what will happen if you show your feelings, most likely as a result of what happened when you were a child. If you showed your dad that you were angry, you were hit across the face or told that you didn't have anything to be angry about. If you showed you were sad, nobody was there to comfort you, to validate that sadness.

Maybe you were told to shut up or you were really going to get something to cry about. The people you loved didn't acknowledge when you were embarrassed; in fact, they may have done things to embarrass you, even to humiliate and shame you. No, it was not safe to show your feelings when you were growing up and, as a result, not only do you avoid expressing your feelings now, but often you don't really know what they are.

I've seen people sit with tears streaming down their faces, clenched fists pounding on the desk, and when asked, "What do you feel?" they respond, "I don't know." It's very common to be so emotionally disconnected from yourself you have difficulty not just showing feelings but identifying them as well.

> ***Common feelings include love, anger, sadness, guilt, embarrassment, fear, loneliness.***

� ***To help you*** explore your feelings, answer the following questions:

- What feelings are easiest for you to show people? Another way of thinking about this is what feelings do you have no difficulty expressing?
- What feelings are more difficult for you to show people? Another way of answering this is what feelings do you have that you would you never want others to see?
- Thinking about those more difficult feelings, what do you fear would happen if you showed them? For example, with fear, what would happen if you let people know you were scared? What do you fear would happen if you told people how lonely you are? What do you fear would happen if you showed your anger? Don't censor your responses; even if you rationally know that's not what would occur, what's the fear?

✦ ***If you are*** inclined to draw or paint or if you are willing to create a collage from words and pictures in magazines, then draw, paint, or create a collage that reflects your answers.

So often the fear of what would happen if we showed our feelings is the echo of what we feared would happen when we were children. It is helpful to ascertain how realistic the fears are today. If they are realistic, what needs to occur for the fears to no longer be valid?

Sadness

If we become sad, we fear that no one will be there to comfort us; people will walk away from us or take advantage of us. They will see us as weak or vulnerable, and that is equated to being bad.

As I said earlier, where there is loss there will be sadness, and where there is sadness there will be tears. Many of us have not cried in a long time. Tears can be very frightening if you have not cried for five, ten, twenty, even thirty years. When that is true, sometimes we are afraid that if we start crying, we will never stop.

I want you to know that your fears about what will happen when you begin to cry are typically *far greater than the reality*. I have often repeated throughout my years of working with clients that nobody yet has had to be carted out of my office because he or she has cried too hard. You may cry for what seems like eternity, but it will only be minutes. The heavy tears last usually three or four minutes, maybe nine or ten. This may make you feel awkward, embarrassed, or afraid because crying may be a strange experience for you, but nothing bad has to happen. You won't die. You won't go crazy.

When people feel emotionally vulnerable and don't want to be with their feelings, their breathing often becomes very shallow. Soon they are breathing from the chest up or, it seems, from the neck up rather than from the gut. Then they get a pain in the back of the ears and feel like they are breathing from the ears out. If this happens to you, it's very important to take slow, deep breaths. Check your breathing. Breathe deeply.

When you cry, you may get flushed in the face. Tears may run down and drip off your nose. That's what happens when people cry. But you are going to feel a sense of relief. You won't have as strong a need to be in control and that will feel good. When the crying is over, you will find you are not carrying so much of the burden of the world on your shoulders any longer.

Anger

In addition to being afraid of sadness and tears, people often fear their anger. Typically, adults with unresolved pain also have a lot of unresolved anger. Some are very much aware of it. Others are so removed from their anger, they are mystified by the thought. People's fears of what would happen should they express anger are, as with sadness, usually *far greater than the reality* of what would occur.

When people become angry, their voices may raise, their faces may get flushed, and their bodies tighten. Fear and sadness may accompany the anger. Angry people who don't express their anger often find it eventually gets expressed directly in unpredicted outbursts, or indirectly in twisted and distorted ways, such as in overeating, insomnia, sarcasm, illness, or violence. Adults who have kept their anger stored away are often afraid they'll become angry people. It's not a matter of becoming. It's a matter of owning. The fear I have heard expressed the most is that these people are afraid they are "going to blow somebody away" with their anger. Most adults don't mean that in the literal sense. When I've asked clients to tell me what that looks like when they "blow someone away," I discover that it most often equates to raising their voices. Yet they have this perception that they have the power to blow someone away.

This perception comes from their childhood. When parents got angry, many children felt as if they were going to be blown away. They felt backed up against a wall and helpless. They may have felt as if their whole life was crumbling because of someone else's response. When someone raised their voice or acted irrationally, the child wanted to disappear. When parents yelled, they didn't talk about behavior; they talked about you, your person, your being. They attacked your whole essence. Of course you felt blown away, especially if this took place when you were developing your sense of worth and identity.

Today, if you disagree with someone, if you need to say no to someone, and if you raise your voice in anger, you have the sense that you are hurting him or her in that same fashion you were hurt as a child. That needs to be put into perspective. At times, you will raise your voice. You will need to say no. You will need to disagree. You can learn to express anger regarding another's behavior without ever attacking another person's identity, value, or essence. You do not have to do to another what was once done to you.

Often there is accumulated anger. Therefore, the anger you may feel at the moment should not be combined with all of the anger you have stored up and then heaped on the immediate source of your anger. It is often helpful to express that anger elsewhere first and then decide whether or not it needs to be directed toward the source. Remember, as you discover your feelings, it is not necessary for you to be alone to figure out how and when to express them. Those who are part of your recovery process can often offer direction. Here are some questions to help you discover your feelings of anger and sadness:

- What picture comes to mind when you visualize yourself showing sadness? Showing anger?
- What old messages were you given about those feelings?
- Are those messages hurting you today? How?
- What new messages can you now create for yourself?

If you were raised in a home where people physically hurt other people, or if in your own adult history you have been physically abusive to yourself or others, the fears concerning your anger are naturally greater and have more basis in reality. To make the process of expressing your anger safer and more meaningful for you, the assistance of a professional counselor who can facilitate your anger work is strongly recommended.

Guilt

It is possible that the fear of exploring the past is not about what will happen if you get in touch with sadness or fear, it is about verifying the guilt you feel over your growing-up years. You still believe there must have been some way you should have been able to influence what happened.

As a child, you could not have known then what you know now. Nor could you have changed what occurred. You must stop trying to take on the responsibility of your growing-up years. You were a child and your experiences were influenced and shaped by others. That is the consequence of childhood.

Some of us find it so hard to believe we really couldn't control what happened in our families. Yet, while we could not control our childhood, we can influence how it impacts who we are today.

Feeling guilty for other people's behaviors and actions is false guilt. Taking on guilt for things over which we had no control is false guilt. There are enough things in life for which we are responsible and therefore can experience true guilt. Believing we were responsible for parental behavior, addictions, compulsions, or believing we should have had the insight or skills of an adult when we were a child or teenager is not among them.

❌ *Do you identify* with experiencing false guilt as a child? If so, describe the situations. Do you still tend to feel guilty for the behavior and actions of others? If so, describe the situations.

Overcoming the Fear of Feelings

Remember, recovery takes time. You don't have to do it all today. When you begin to tell people of your awkwardness or your fears, they won't seem so overwhelming. Feelings are only hurtful when they are denied, minimized, and when they accumulate.

Know that in the early stages of healing, your feelings will arise from many sources and some may seem very contrary to each other. You may feel sad and happy at the same time, or sad and angry, or loving and hateful. It is possible for all of us to have many contradictory feelings at the same time. You have not gone crazy. It only means you're sad and happy, sad and angry, or that you love and you hate.

Also, trust that there are reasons for the depth of your feelings. Whatever you feel doesn't mean you are bad. What's important is that you are able to talk about those feelings and that you begin to put them out in front of somebody else. You don't have to know the sources of your feelings. But you can open your mouth and say, "I'm sad. I don't know what's going on, but I feel sad." The more you verbalize what you do know and what you feel, the sooner you'll be able to connect your feelings to the sources.

The goal in this process is to be able to discover and acknowledge the reality of what has been lost, to feel the feelings associated with the loss(es). To do this requires support and a willingness to relinquish the emotional maneuvers that you have used to deny this reality. You need to be able to admit that the loss is permanent. You will never experience the ideal that you so desperately wished for in childhood. While you can do much today to get many of those needs met, no amount of experience or grieving will completely erase how it was "then." Ultimately, this allows you to be willing to withdraw your emotional investment in what has been lost and move on in your recovery process.

It is usually early in the discovery process that the pain may seem overwhelming, but it will pass if you are willing to identify and own it. It is very important that you have a support system, people you can talk with regularly about these feelings. Talking, rather than keeping the feelings within, often takes the power out of the feelings. Receiving validation from others lessens the pain as well.

As you begin to experience these pent-up feelings from the past, go ahead and fully feel those feelings. As intense as the pain can be, trying to control and defend those feelings prolongs the pain. Allow yourself the feelings. Own them and be with them. Remember that a lot of what you are experiencing is the accumulation of many years of feelings—feelings that previously were not safe to experience. This does take time, but people who actively pursue self-discovery in a therapy or self-help environment find that usually within six to eight months the pain has greatly lessened. In those times of great feeling, you may need to take deliberate steps to lessen external stresses. This is no time to take on added responsibilities. Make more time for yourself. Stay aware that this is a vulnerable time—it is a passage that does not last forever. Now is the time to treat yourself with kindness.

Exploring your past and grieving the pain associated with your losses is vital to recovery, but it is just as important to move beyond this first step. If not, you will become stuck in the process and it will then become a blaming process, not a grief process.

Talking about your childhood is not the complete answer to changing the course of your life. This is a time of much insight, awareness, and understanding of yourself and others. It is a time of hope, a time of realizing that you have greater choices available. Hopefully, the talking and new awareness will bring you to your turning point. But once you reach that point, you must take three other steps that are vital for your recovery.

Step Two: Connect the Past to Present Life

"How Does This Past Loss Influence Who I Am Today?"

Connecting your past to the present is more of a rational, insight-oriented process than an emotional process. The cause-and-effect connections you discover between your past losses and present life will give you a sense of direction. This clarity will identify the areas you need to work on—where pain still affects you, where you are missing the skills needed to get free of the influences and restrictions from the past.

As you work on answering the question, "How does my past affect who I am today?" you become increasingly centered in the here and now. Also, you will need to address that question to various areas of your life, such as:

- How does my past affect who I am as a parent?
- How does that affect who I am in the workplace?
- How does that affect who I am in a relationship?
- How does that affect how I feel about myself?

These are questions you seldom take time to ask yourself, but the answers are vital in your recovery. It is helpful to take the time to write your responses. Growing up with shame, you had a tendency to intellectualize most things. Through writing you may find yourself more vulnerable and, as a result, more honest. And as you work on this step in your recovery, you need to make each question even more detailed. Here are examples of the general questions becoming more specific to your life today:

1. How does the fact that I lived with chronic loneliness for the first twenty years of my life affect how I feel about myself today?
2. How does that affect me in the context of my relationships? Friendships? In my parenting skills?

3. How does the fact that I was so fearful of making mistakes in my childhood affect me today in my work? In my play? As a parent?
4. How does the fact that, as a child, I was always seeking approval affect me today in my parenting? In my relationships? At work?
5. How does the fact that I spent so much of my childhood in isolation and a fantasy world as a child affect me today? In my expectations of myself? My choice of friends?
6. How does the fact that the only way I could find safety was to create a fantasy world affect me in my choice of careers?
7. How does the fact that I lived with chronic fear affect me today in these areas of my life?
8. How does the fact that it was never safe to express my anger affect me in these areas?
9. How does the fact that I lived with a mother who was emotionally cold, a father who was never satisfied with what I did, affect me today?

These are the kinds of questions you need to ask yourself and that create a cause-and-effect connection between your childhood years and your life today.

We often make assumptions about one of the areas of our lives without going through the exploration process. For example, we may assume that since "work is good," and "I am doing a good job," we don't need to explore that area. But, by asking ourselves these questions in Step Two, by linking the past to how we function in the present, often we discover ways that we continue to perpetuate pain or repeat old behaviors that hinder rather than help us. By asking, "How does the fact that I used school and keeping busy to detract from my loneliness relate to my work today?" we may find that we are presently using work as the detractor that school once was. We may work sixteen hours every day for weeks and then reward ourselves by going on a food or alcohol binge or a spending binge, seemingly to reward ourselves for a job well done. Very likely we did do a good job at work, but what we have done even better is add to our load of shame—another ten pounds gained, another drunk-driving ticket, another outrageous credit card debt, and a closet full of clothes we don't need or really want.

While this step connecting the past and present offers us insight, it also will bring up feelings. For instance, think about what it means to be forty-five years old today and still afraid to make a decision. How does that make you feel about your adequacy? Further, what if you haven't learned to listen? How has that interfered in relationships with intimate partners? What do you feel when you try to identify your needs? The answers to such questions bring up a lot of pain.

Kate, a client, reflected, "It was so hard to be with my pain because I realized the fantasy life I created for myself as a child has been what has kept me so unrealistic in terms of my life goals. I realized it never felt safe to make a decision, and that is still true today!" We are often grateful to understand the past-present connection and find it useful to be able to recognize how old messages and experiences still dictate our lives. Yet, we also need to own the anger we may have about that or the sadness that accompanies the insight or even the fear that comes with now wanting to change certain patterns.

We need to connect the past to the present. And, as we do that, we need to feel the feelings, identify the source of the feelings, and grieve the pain.

Step Three: Challenge Internalized Beliefs

"What Are the Beliefs I Internalized from My Growing-Up Years?"
"Are Those Beliefs Helpful or Hurtful to Me Today?"
"What Beliefs Do I Want to Have Today?"

Beliefs we internalized in our growing-up years often continue to determine our behaviors without our being aware. These messages were often parental attitudes and value statements that became shoulds. First, we need to identify the beliefs, and then we need to ask ourselves whether these messages are positive or negative, helpful or hurtful to how we want to live our life today. We need to question whether or not these internalized messages are messages that we want to continue to take with us throughout our adulthood.

So, we begin this step asking, "What do I believe about_____?" and then we must challenge our answers: "Is that a belief that is helpful to me today?" or "Is that a belief that is harmful to me now?"

Examples of beliefs we often learned at a young age that are hurtful to us are:

- I can't trust anybody.
- Nobody is ever going to be there for me.
- I am not important.
- I am not of value.
- I better do things right because if I don't, something bad is going to happen.
- My needs are not important. Everyone else's are far more important.
- There's no time to play. I have to get things done.
- I am *supposed* to take care of others.
- I can't do anything, so I don't bother.
- Whatever I do, it's never good enough.
- Other _____

> ✷ *Return to the* list and put a check by the beliefs from which you operate. Name additional beliefs that were formed from your experience that are hurtful now.

These hurtful, internalized messages interfere with skill-building. For example, if you truly believe your needs aren't important, it will be difficult to learn to express your needs. If you believe you can't do anything or what you do is never good enough, you won't initiate or try anything new on your own. If you believe your job is to take care of others, you will very likely neglect yourself. It's going to be important to identify a certain message and to decide—to choose—whether or not this is a message you want to keep.

Once hurtful messages are identified, you need to symbolically let them go. Many adults changing course skip over this part of the step. They explore the past, they connect the past to the present, they try to learn some skills, but they don't actively look at the messages they have internalized. And sometimes when they do look at a message and identify it, they don't actively get rid of it.

There are many ways to symbolically get rid of an old belief.

> ✷ *Develop a ritual* that works for you. For example:

- Write the belief down and tear it up.
- Write it down on a piece of poster paper, put it in a chair, and say no to it.
- Do a visualization of the belief; that is, visualize the belief and watch it disintegrate.
- If you play computer games, put the piece of paper with the belief on it into a playing field and bomb it.

It is important for you to get actively involved in letting the belief go. The purpose is serious, but the process can be fun. After the ritual of letting go of the old belief, replace it with a healthy message. Here are some examples of old, unchallenged beliefs replaced with beliefs you choose.

Old Inaccurate Belief	**New Revised Belief**
People aren't trustworthy.	Most people can be trusted.
I have to say yes.	Saying no can be a healthy boundary.
There is no time to play.	Time to play is important.
Mistakes mean I'm a failure.	Mistakes mean I'm only human.

Although you need to replace negative beliefs, you probably received some helpful messages from your family. It will be just as important to ascertain what those were. You may have heard from your father that you were special, of value. Or that you could do whatever it is that you wanted to do (high expectations). You may have heard the Golden Rule: "Do unto others as you want them to do unto you." Many times these are messages that you would like to continue to take with you in life. When that is true, you need to take ownership of the beliefs.

You need to know what *you* believe, not just your father's (or mother's) belief system that you have internalized. You need to literally say, "That's what my father told me and that's been very helpful to me. Now I believe that for myself." You don't need to hear them just as your father's message for you. You will take ownership of the message, the belief. "I am capable, I am special, I am of value, and I can do whatever I set my mind to doing." The baton has been turned over to you, so to speak, and you are now responsible for carrying this message.

Once you have discovered any parental beliefs or shoulds you have internalized that are getting in the way of how you want to live your life, toss them out. But again, know that while this begins as more of an intellectual search, you will have feelings that need to be felt. Identifying that you have lived a life believing "My needs aren't important" is something to be angry about. Recognizing that you have experienced "No one wants to listen to what I have to say" is very sad. As you reframe a healthier message in the place of the old message, you must work through the emotions of change.

Be thorough as you work on this step because it is the one people are most likely to skip over and neglect. It can appear insignificant or trivial. In general, a strong emotional reaction is not created, so there is not the level of excitement some people expect in recovery. Depending on which issue you are addressing, it can be very emotionally loaded, but that is not the main idea of this step. The point is that it is vital to address your issues and take more responsibility for how you live your life today.

It is in working on these three steps that you are ready to truly learn and incorporate new behaviors or skills into your life.

Step Four: Learn New Skills

"What Do I Want to Do Differently Today?"

Ultimately, our life changes when we learn skills or behaviors—things we can learn to do to take care of ourselves and to have healthy relationships with others—that we didn't learn in our earlier years. "I want to be a better listener," "I want to learn to solve problems better," "I want to be able to see options," "I want to learn to negotiate better." These are living skills and people skills, ways of being with yourself and with others.

People will often want to bypass the first three steps and simply get on with learning new skills. Most of us are in a hurry to move on in our lives, and that is understandable. Ever since childhood, we have been anxious to leave the present moment in anticipation of the next day. We were certain the next day had to be better. We don't want to grieve or to take time to be insightful about connecting the past to the present or to spend time doing what appears to be a trivial exercise of challenging our beliefs. We have other things to do. But we must be willing to prioritize our recovery. That means taking the time to walk through each step of the process.

You can immerse yourself in programs that focus solely on behavioral change. However, most people find that if they do not do each step in successive order, they won't follow through with practicing the new skill because they have not addressed the emotional component to each skill.

Let's say, for example, that you want to do a better job of setting limits for yourself. You want to be more assertive because you are feeling victimized in certain situations. But what happens is this: You can learn assertiveness techniques and skills, but very likely you won't follow through and actually use those skills because you haven't dealt with the issues of the fear of rejection and the need for approval. Those are the emotional issues connected to the skill.

Or you want to learn how to ask others for help. You can identify safe people, develop a behavioral hierarchy identifying a list of items or issues to ask for help with, but unless you deal with how frightening it was to ask for help as a child, you won't follow through with practicing the new skill.

Your intellect or rational mind will now know what to do to bring about the result you want, but your underlying emotions will impede you from choosing to act in that new way. The new behavior won't follow until the emotional component underlying the old behavior has been dealt with. That's what happens in the first three steps—you deal with those old beliefs and fears. You then create a new belief system that supports the new behavior, the new skill you want to learn.

As you change course, you go through a process where ultimately you withdraw your emotional investment in what has been lost and take responsibility for taking care of and respecting yourself. This self-care and self-respect is created by developing and reframing beliefs that are supportive of your emotional and physical health, and then by learning the skills that act on these new beliefs, taking personal responsibility for getting your needs met.

Learning Adult Skills as a Child
Children in troubled families do learn skills. In fact, sometimes they learn skills that other children don't. Some learn to cook at a particularly young

age. Others become very skilled at controlling their emotions. In their hyper-vigilance many develop strong listening skills. They also become creative in their problem-solving and self-reliant.

Often we were responding to situations as if we had the skills of an adult, but we were still children. Unfortunately, the skills we learned in a troubled home were often skills and behaviors that were premature for our age or learned from a basis of fear or shame. When that occurs, there is a tendency to feel like an imposter. Also, because we developed skills from a premise of fear or shame and because we learned due to an immediate need, we were often limited in options and problem-solving. This commonly translates to being rigid in how we handle situations as adults.

So now, while we have skills, we don't have flexibility. We have a sense of urgency about what we're doing: "I had better do this, and I'd better do it right. I can't make a mistake, because if I do, something bad is going to happen." We are skilled, but we feel a sense of urgency with fear and shame close behind.

It is important to take a look at the skills you did learn. Be open to developing those even more fully with the input of healthier role models to whom you have access today.

To help you begin to look at your own experience, here are some of the behaviors or skills children need to learn.

- Asking for help.
- Expressing feelings appropriately.
- Setting limits.
- Saying no.
- Validating self.
- Initiating
- Asking questions.
- Negotiating.
- Problem-solving.
- Taking charge.
- Listening.
- Playing.

❖ *List the skills* you developed growing up. Then list the skills that you did not develop. Usually these skills are very basic but are vital today in being able to address more complex skills in adult life.

Adult skills are often taken for granted, except by those who may not have had the opportunity to develop them. If we did not learn these skills as a child and adolescent, we move into adulthood forced to experience ourselves as if we were an imposter. We try to hide our performance anxiety, fear of change, and fear of problem-solving, spending a great amount of time and energy manipulating our environment so we don't have to be confronted with what we perceive to be our "insufficiency." But, often we didn't know or didn't understand there was another way to be.

Recovery offers you the opportunity to acknowledge what you need to learn.

↳ To say, "I did not learn this basic skill, and I need to know it," is a turning point.

Feelings Associated with Learning New Skills

Learning new skills is much more behavioral than emotional, yet like the other steps there will be associated feelings. You will experience feelings as you identify and recover from the ways you have been trying to control your pain from the past. Also, you will have other feelings, such as awkwardness and unfamiliarity as you try your new skills and as you relate to other people in your newly discovered ways.

Having to go back to learn basic skills at this point in your life brings up a lot of different, painful emotions. Each and every possible time you have a feeling, you must stop, pay attention to it—honor it. You need to

1. feel the feeling,
2. identify the source of the feeling, and
3. express it in the here and now.

You will need to go through this process consciously until doing so becomes habit, until you consistently meet your own needs.

Here are some pertinent questions to think about to help bring your feelings to the surface:

- If you are just now in the process of learning to make decisions, how does it make you feel having to learn that skill now? Afraid? Angry? Sad?
- If you are just now learning to listen to your significant others—family, friends, and intimate partner—how do you feel about the problems that were created by your inability to be open to hearing them? Sad? Guilty? Regretful?
- When you try now to identify your own needs, how does that make you feel? Confused? Insecure? Uncertain? Afraid?
- Not knowing your own needs surely means these needs weren't being met. As a result, your neediness may affect your present-day relationships. What feelings do you now have about trying to have your needs met in your relationships? Fear? Confusion? Insecurity?

Each of the feelings you name as you answer these questions includes a lot of pain. When you begin to practice the skills that allow you to take care of yourself, you often feel as vulnerable as a child who is just learning to read. You are no longer that child and so you do not want to tell yourself you "should" be able to do these things. Remember, this is not about "shoulds." Maybe it was not safe when you were growing up to have learned a certain skill, such as assertiveness. Or perhaps there were no models of this skill to learn from. Whatever your circumstances, you coped and survived as best as you could, and it was not until later in life that you could recognize that you lacked these kinds of skills.

Applying the Four Steps to a Recovery Issue

Each and every issue in your recovery process will usually be addressed by these four steps. Let's use as an example that *saying no* is a problem for you now because of what you experienced around the word *no* as a child. Here's what your process might look like.

Step One: Explore past losses.

> How did you hear *no* as a child?
> Who did you hear it from?
> What did that experience mean to you as a reflection of your worth?
> What happened when you said *no* as a child?
> How did that make you feel?

Step Two: Connect the past to the present.

> How does your past experience affect you in the different areas of your life today?
> When do you have difficulty saying *no*?
> How do you feel when you say *no?*

Step Three: Challenge internalized beliefs.

> What were the messages you got around *no?*
> Take ownership of the helpful beliefs.
> Cast out the hurtful messages.
> Create new, constructive beliefs around the word *no.*

Step Four: Learn new skills.

> Identify situations when you would like to say *no.*
> Rank these from easiest to most difficult.
> Practice the experience of saying *no,* beginning with the easiest and build up to most difficult.

In the example above, the four steps were applied to the problem of saying *no.* Here is another example of using the four steps, applied to difficulty in initiating.

Step One: Explore past losses.

> What happened if you tried to initiate as a child?
> What did you fear would happen?

Step Two: Connect the past to the present.

> How does not initiating today impact you in different areas of your life?

What could you have in your life today if you did initiate?

Step Three: Challenge internalized beliefs.

As a child, what messages did you get about initiating?

Cast out the hurtful messages.

Create new beliefs that support you taking initiative versus being passive.

Step Four: Learn new skills.

Identify areas in which you would like to take more initiative.

List identified skills in a hierarchy, beginning with those that are the easiest (or safest) to those that are the most difficult or scariest.

Now begin with the safest, building up confidence to be able to respond to the most difficult.

Recovery Can't Be Rushed

Be kind to yourself. Give yourself credit. Remember, as you work the recovery process, you are working through the four steps to greater freedom.

↳ Recovery isn't changing who you are. It is letting go of who you are not.

Chapter Four

Building Your Own
Inner Adult

Skills to Create a Core of Personal Strength

"Owning our story and loving ourselves through that process is the bravest thing that we will ever do."

—Brené Brown

"It is in knowing what your needs are that they are most apt to be met."
—Claudia Black

Tony described himself as having this crippling fear of women. He saw women as controlling and intrusive and didn't want to give them a chance. In therapy he reflected, "My mother was everywhere and nowhere at the same time. She controlled everything about my life. 'Where are you going? What are you reading? You need to be doing this now, that now.' Everything, yet, in truth, she wasn't really ever there for me."

Hannah reflected, "My father was drunk the day I was born. By that time he was well into 'the hates.' My dad turned a lot of his self-loathing outward. He'd show up at school assemblies and shout obscenities at the nuns. Sometimes during our priest's sermon at Sunday mass, I'd hear my dad's unmistakable voice at the back of the church. He'd be talking too loudly, swearing at the priest. I felt ashamed, as if his outbursts were my fault. It took away my dignity."

These two accounts describe the kinds of family environments where children's personal boundaries and core identities are threatened at very young ages, when they are just beginning to develop a sense of a personal self and self-worth. The questions children must struggle to answer are universal and central to all of us:

- "Who am I? Am I an extension of my mother, a possession of my father, or a real and separate individual?"
- "How much am I worth? Am I loved? Am I lovable?"
- "What do I think and feel? What happens when I tell my parents my secret fears?"
- "When can I say no? Or do I always have to say yes in order to be loved? For if I am not loved, surely I will be abandoned, and if I am abandoned, surely I will die."

These central questions create our sense of self and the answers we settle on are determined largely by the responses from those around us. In situations like those above and in countless other families, children are given negative answers, mixed messages, or no answers at all, which may be the most devastating kind of parental response. Without answers from those we love and depend on for survival, the questions are left to echo in our dark interior self until we attempt through our own childhood logic to guess at an answer.

Creating an Inner Holding Environment

Although the specifics are different in everyone's lives, we do know a great deal about the dynamics that are common within troubled families. We know that something, some event or some force, has disrupted the natural order of lives. An event might be the absence/loss of a parent through death or divorce, a parent's debilitating depression, or drastically reduced living conditions for the family. A force might be as blatantly harmful as drug addiction, or subtle and deceptively benign—a strict religious code of behavior, for example.

In the midst of chaos, rigidity, or a combination of the extremes, and in the absence of strong, positive parental messages to the contrary, children conclude that they are not of value and that they may at any time be abandoned. These two things in combination are the source of almost unbearable shame.

We are often desperate in our attempts to hide our core self because we feel damaged or loathsome. Unbeknown to us, other children had early daily encounters with loving, nurturing mothers and fathers, so they felt both physically and emotionally safe. They were able to internalize memories of being cared for, which then formed their core beliefs about and behaviors toward themselves. These core beliefs and behaviors are the ones we will have to learn on our own because, as Judith Viorst writes, "We cannot stand alone until we come to possess this inner holding environment." The core beliefs and behaviors that create this inner holding environment are the core recovery skills built around a core of positive regard for ourselves and the willingness to nurture our inner being.

Core Recovery Skills

New awareness of what is possible can bring you to the turning point in your life. You can change course. It is important to remember, though, that you are not changing *who* you are. You are changing certain beliefs and behaviors—you are changing how you see yourself and how you take care of your pain!

Using the Four Steps to Recovery discussed in Chapter Three, you will have a basic understanding of how your past has been affecting your life and how you can challenge and change old beliefs and behaviors for your present and future. Now you are ready to learn the skills you need to take care of yourself on your course to recovery.

Core Recovery Skills
1. Validate yourself.

2. Let go of some control.
3. Feel your feelings.
4. Identify your needs.
5. Set limits and boundaries.

These are the skills everyone needs but which you did not learn because, whether all or in part, these were missing when you were growing up. Because you did not receive validation, you did not feel of value. With a child's logic, you concluded that you were not worthy. During the very early stages of your development, and without other messages to the contrary, there was no way for you to conclude anything else. The family is the be all and end all to children's experiences until they get old enough and mature enough to conceive of other possibilities.

When chaos prevailed—because of a raging alcoholic or because parents were literally absent in the home for whatever reason—your physical survival was in jeopardy. When rigidity was the order, your emotional survival, and possibly your physical survival, were at risk since severe punishment often followed misbehavior. Whatever the case in your family, whether it be chaos, rigidity, or some other extreme, the first priority was, literally, to save yourself. So you tried in every way possible to be in control of what happened to you and others who were at risk.

Of course, when you were discounted, shamed, or punished, you simply hid your feelings, and then kept hiding them deeper and deeper until you didn't seem to feel them anymore. Along with no longer recognizing your own feelings, you also learned to ignore your needs. After all, your parents' needs and wants came first. If your parents or others in your family were sucked into a system of addiction and codependency, children were simply caught up in following the rules of protection and denial, as well as caretaking the parents and themselves. If the central dynamic of the system was some kind of obsession with a religious code, children's needs were probably not acknowledged as legitimate and any deviance from that code was a sin.

Whatever was true in your family, others set your limits and tried to invade the boundaries of your core self and perhaps the boundaries of your physical self. Inevitably, these intrusions were confusing and painful.

Today you are, in essence, becoming your own parent. In truth, we all parent ourselves when we become adults. We have internalized beliefs and behaviors that either echo our parents or stand in opposition to them, as we try to compensate for the negative effects we felt. Rather than look back in anger at what we did and didn't learn, or look with envy at what others did learn, we can simply begin with the premise that all of us act as either loving or unloving parents to ourselves now.

Parenting ourselves is a concept that feels artificial to some and off-putting to others—maybe because we have negative memories of being parented and so that's the last thing we want to go through again. However, let's not get stuck in the connotations of the words *parent* and *child*. Let's just take a careful look at how we treat ourselves. We either put ourselves down or build ourselves up; we treat ourselves badly or we take care of ourselves. But now, we can consciously decide what we want to do for ourselves or, if you will, what kind of parent we want to be. We can decide what we want to believe and feel and do about ourselves—and go from there.

"Gradualness"

Taking steps one at a time is a natural learning process that builds on itself. If we jump into situations before we learn how to handle them we won't be able to reach our goals. For example, we may hope to have intimacy in our relationships but we may not have learned yet how to express our feelings. Or, we want to be the perfect parent but we never learned how to set limits for ourselves, let alone our children. However, rather than being hard on ourselves for wanting too much, too soon, we can remind ourselves that rebuilding our lives requires gradualness. Being raised in a troubled family often meant being raised in a family where your sense of safety was unsure. You couldn't trust that you were going to be physically protected. Because of that, you didn't feel psychologically safe. You didn't feel the protection that children need to experience in order to be willing to risk assertive behavior. You didn't feel the protection children need to experience to be willing to risk sharing what they feel and need. Safety to share and to risk are elements that nurture a person's growth. It is my hope that as you change course now, you will find recovery to be a safe process. That does not mean your life will be pain-free or necessarily easy, but that you will feel safe to risk and grow.

There are different ways people approach recovery, just as there are different ways to learn other skills. Take swimming, as an example. If I wanted to teach children to swim there are many ways to do that. It is possible to take children out on a raft in water ten feet over their heads, throw them over the side, and expect them to swim back to shore. While many children would make it back to shore, it is very possible a few would not and would be in danger of drowning. This is a harsh and unnecessary way to learn.

The recovery process does not need to be so harsh. Don't be in a rush to jump into recovery situations that are ten feet over your head. When you've learned and acquired core recovery skills you will have built the foundation for your inner holding environment. Practicing these skills will allow you to face the core causes of your pain without feeling like you will drown in your emotions. It is as if you are learning to swim with a sense of safety, starting in shallow waters and developing your self-confidence as you go deeper.

It is my hope that early on in recovery you quickly begin to practice self-validation and self-approval. This paves the way for you to feel safer as you explore more fully the issues of control, confronting your need to stay in control and learning to let go little by little. Letting go of control quickly results in immediately being thrust into the issue of dealing with powerful feelings. At the point you begin to identify and express feelings you will also start to identify your needs. Then, to get needs met, you must begin to set limits and boundaries. As you do these things, you are developing a sense of self—a sense of who you really are. Self-worth is increasing. Shame is lessening. A foundation of positive self-regard is being constructed.

This foundation will offer you the safety to go to greater depths within yourself, which in turn will take you further on the course of your recovery. As you proceed to build the strength of your inner core you will undoubtedly still be frightened of letting go of some control. With this and other difficult issues, I want you to have some comfort with your feelings. If you start to cry, I want you to know that you are not going crazy. And if you are angry, you don't have to self-destruct. I want you also to be able to identify what you need.

Very often people feel the need to jump into all of their issues at once, and that is like experiencing emotional or cognitive surgery without medical help or preparation. When this occurs, the consequences are so frightening that people often just stop their efforts to work through their pain. They may become so afraid of what they are feeling that they won't risk continuing. By taking steps one at a time, the gradualness provides the safety to continue in the process. At the same time, these recovery skills can't really be worked on in a totally compartmentalized fashion. You cannot do all the work that is necessary in one area—validating yourself, for example—before moving on to another skill, such as identifying your needs. Human emotions are not that simple, and human behavior is not constant or absolute. Our issues will easily overlap and working through them will require different skills in different combinations. Yet, when we set out to learn the skills, the concept of doing the steps of recovery in order is still valid.

Validating Yourself

We need to gain a sense of value in order to feel we are worthy of the recovery process. As soon as possible, we must begin the process of actively valuing and approving ourselves.

A part of recovery is to become independent of the need for other people's approval. Many people raised in troubled families are often highly dependent upon others' approval and on what others think of them. It is important to become self-validating so that we are not so dependent on others, but also because it allows us to see movement in our process of recovery. It allows us to see that, in fact, we are doing things differently now than we have done them in the past. It allows us to see our progress, and that gives us something to celebrate. It also gives us a sense of hope, direction, and helps to keep us in the process.

Yet, most of us are harshly critical of ourselves. Unless we do something as significant as moving a mountain, it is never good enough. And then if we do move the mountain, unless there are people there applauding, it is still never good enough. Few people in their lifetimes ever move mountains, but if they do, they do it with the help of a lot of other people and by taking a lot of little steps. However, it isn't the mountain getting moved that makes the difference—it is the little steps along the way.

Earlier I mentioned the tendency for people to take recovery in leaps and bounds. This is understandable because so much of your life has been experienced in extremes and with unrealistic expectations. You have often lived your life from a "one and ten" perspective (forgetting the numbers two through nine)—an all-or-nothing way of being, feeling, living.

ϟ Recovery is learning the numbers two through nine.

We need to accept and validate ourselves for being who we are. Because we can never be perfect, we are not doomed to failure. We must accept both our power and powerlessness in life.

We deserve to experience our personal growth, to celebrate and feel good about ourselves. Yet, it is so difficult to be self-approving when, as a child, you learned that no matter what you did, it was never good enough. We don't need anyone today to reinforce this belief/delusion; we have internalized it. We have been constantly repeating that message to ourselves. As children we needed our parents to tell us specifically what was likable or lovable about us. We needed our parents to applaud us for just being. Parents are often critical of their children, very abrupt in their responses, and often simply don't notice the little things (or even the big things) that help children feel good about who they are.

One child comes home from school, looking forward to telling her mother about the day, to find Mom passed out on the couch. Another child comes home to tell his mother something that made him feel good that day and finds Mom locked inside the bedroom crying. In either case, the children aren't going to be acknowledged, supported, or validated. Their needs are ignored, and they are recognized only when they try to take care of their mother.

Another child brings home his report card that shows he has done extremely well. He is anxious to show it to Dad, seeking Dad's approval, but Dad doesn't come home that night. In fact, three days go by before Dad returns. Do you think anyone remembers then that this thirteen-year-old boy has brought home his report card? Does anyone care? No, everybody is focused on Dad—where he had been, what he was doing, and what will happen now.

When children are developing their sense of worth and their identity, they gain a sense of their personal value by others' verbal responses, or failure to respond, and others' behavior toward them. Children need to know what is good about their behavior and themselves. "I need to know that I am special. I am of value. I am important." They consistently need to hear words that affirm this. When that does not occur, children fail to internalize a sense of worth, value, or accomplishment.

As an adult, you need to begin validating yourself as a part of your own reparenting process. When people truly begin to validate themselves simply for being who they are, they are not going to have to continue to seek outside approval.

When you first begin to look back at your early loss conditions, such as the absence of validation, it is easy to get overwhelmed by personal pain. Consequently, people often comment they wish they were still in denial. People talk about entering the tunnel of recovery and, rather than seeing light at the end, feel the tunnel closing in around them, getting darker. If this happens to you, it may help to remember this:

   ↳   By recognizing that you are in the process of recovery, you are beginning to shine your own light.

You deserve to have a sense of moving forward. You deserve self-validation and self-approval. This will give you a sense of hope and give you the patience you deserve to help you work through your losses.

I want you to be able to validate yourself so you can say:

- "Today someone asked my opinion and I had one. Yes, me! I—who have never felt safe forming my own opinion—I had one."
- "Today I got angry and I knew it. In the past it took me six years to figure out I had a feeling and another two years to know it was anger."
- "I didn't work through my whole lunch hour, just half of it."
- "Today I received a compliment. I said thank you and didn't say, 'Yes, but . . .'"

Affirming, approving, validating—these are the little steps for which you deserve applause. It is very important to stop and take time to identify the little steps in recovery, the little bits of success. This strengthens your sense of self and reinforces your new beliefs. Also, try not to be preoccupied with what hasn't changed for you yet. Focus on what is happening now.

 ❖ *Identify at least* two steps you are taking in your own recovery. Take it in. Allow yourself to feel good that there is movement. Let go of any "buts." Little steps may be, "I am reading this book." "I am allowing myself to take in a compliment and not reject it." I am pausing before I respond to people when they have said something that hurt or confused me." "I take a walk a few times a week." Remember, you are looking for *little* steps.

 ❖ *As a way* of making self-validation a habit, take time out each day to focus on your positive attributes. Recognize at least two new behaviors or attitudes.

Here is an example of the four recovery steps applied to self-validation.

Step One
Describe how validation was or was not experienced in your growing-up years.
How did that feel?
Be willing to feel the pain associated with those experiences.

Step Two
Identify how the experience you had regarding validation in your growing-up years has affected your willingness and ability to self-validate today.

Step Three
Identify specific beliefs you have internalized about the act of self-validation.
Are these beliefs hurtful or helpful to you today?

Identify the ones you want to let go of and those you would like to maintain.

Step Four

Begin to practice the skill of validating yourself, for example, by repeating, "I am a whole human being with a wide range of thoughts and feelings.

I accept and love myself—my body, my thoughts, my feelings— just the way that I am, and I know that I am worthy."

Affirmations

Affirmations are important to the healing process. They are statements of acceptance that encourage the manifestation of your healing journey. Being repetitious with affirmations helps to create a neurochemical change that reinforces acceptance of the belief. When doing an affirmation:

- Be positive, never use negatives in affirmations.
- Don't discount. Act "as if." The more you accept the possibilities, the stronger the affirmation.
- Write them. As you are learning to do affirmations write them down so you will remember exactly what you want to say.
- Keep them short and specific.
- Keep them in the present, not the future.

Examples:
- I deserve to be treated respectfully.
- I am responsible for my life.
- I am courageous.
- My mistakes make me human.
- I am lovable.
- I love my body.

✖ *Make a list* of affirmations that are true for you. Keep them with you at all times. Periodically, throughout the day, pull them out and say them. Get to the point that you don't need your list but can draw upon the skill of spontaneously acknowledging that which you can feel good about.

Letting Go of Some Control

Most of us adults know a lot about the word *control,* but those of us raised in either chaotic or rigid environments know very little about the word *some*—S-O-M-E, as in "some control." To us, control has been something we either have or we don't. The concept of "some control" has seemed as impossible as being "a little bit pregnant."

Perceiving control to be an all-or-nothing experience, naturally we don't want to give it up. That would be the same, we believe, as being "out of control." Also, we don't want to give up control because it once protected us. Giving up control is frightening because it has been vital to our sense of safety. Control of the external forces in your environment is a survival mechanism. It may be self-protection in a physical sense. Or, from the standpoint of your beliefs and feelings, control is what allowed you, when you were a young child, to make sense out of your life. Controlling behavior is an attempt to bring order and consistency into inconsistent and unpredictable family situations. Controlling behavior is a defense against shame. Feeling a sense of control gives children a sense of power at a time in their lives when they are overwhelmed with powerlessness, helplessness, and fears. Giving up control as an adult is difficult when, up to this point in life, it has been of great value.

One way children learn control is by manipulating their environment. They try to control the aspects of their lives that are tangible or concrete. You can see this when children act as their own parent, and/or as the parent to their brothers and sisters. Sometimes they act as a parent to their mother and father.

Angel said she actually used to discipline herself for having misbehaved. "I would do things and not be reprimanded. I talked back to my parents. I would swear. Maybe I would be late for school. So I would discipline myself. I put myself on restriction. I would role-play verbal reprimands. I used television shows as my guide. I actually raised myself fairly well."

At eleven years of age, Tim was the one who set the bedtime for his younger brother and sister. He made sure they had a bath before they went to bed. He literally tucked them in himself. He then made sure their lunches were made before school the next morning.

Fourteen-year-old Kimberly used to call her father to tell him what he needed to do before he came home from work. This same youngster was the one who covered her mother up after she passed out on the couch, so that she wouldn't get too cold during the middle of the night.

Ten-year-old Paul put the car in the garage every night when his dad would leave it running in the middle of the front yard. He didn't want the neighbors to think there was anything wrong at his house.

These are examples of children trying their best to create order and safety in their lives.

> ✖ *Were you one* of those children who exerted this type of control? If so, describe. Does this type of behavior get in the way of your life today?

While many children try to control that which is external—people, places, and things—they may also attempt to control internal, intangible aspects of their personal lives. Some children become very controlling by withholding their feelings. Discounting their feelings usually goes along with this.

"I'm not angry. What's there to be angry about? I've seen it before."

"I wasn't embarrassed. I'm used to those things by now."

"No, I didn't feel sad. Last time I cried, they called me names."

Some children become very controlling by diminishing their own needs, neither expecting nor asking for anything.

"I don't need to go to my friend's house. Who would be home to take care of my sister?"

"I don't want a birthday party. Dad wouldn't show up anyway."

"I don't want my mom to come to the PTA meeting. Last time she showed up, it was a major fiasco."

Diminishing needs and withholding feelings are invisible, internal controlling mechanisms. This is self-control, protection to ward off further pain by repressing desires and feelings.

Some children become very controlling through withdrawal and isolation. They go off in the corner and read. They daydream in their bedroom or, when teenagers, spend as little time at home as possible. They establish a social boundary that says, "Stay away. I don't need you. I don't want you. Let me go do something alone in safety that keeps me from the depth of my painful feelings."

> ✦ *Do you identify* with the description of being an internal controller? If so, describe. Does that get in the way of your life today?

Because of their early experiences, people do differ in the depth of their control and in the ways they control. However, in my work, I have consistently observed some commonalities.

1. The greater the physical and emotional chaos in a family, the greater a child will find the need for control in every area of his or her life.
2. The faster the dysfunction in a family progresses and deepens, the less a child becomes an external controller and instead becomes more of an internal controller.
3. When another family member is already an external controller, there is less need for another child to be an external controller, so more often that child will learn to control internally only.
4. External controllers also control internally, but some people are only internal controllers.

When we were children, our attempts to control, whether internally or externally, were about survivorship. It made sense in the context of our environment.

Unfortunately, the continued need for control causes problems in our adult lives. We have spent years being hyper-vigilant, manipulating others and ourselves as a way of protection. Now we literally don't know how to live life differently. We don't have any idea why we would want to live life differently. Because we have survived, our ways have apparently been right.

Sadly, however, because we have become so encapsulated and narrow in our view of the world, we don't see what others can so readily see— that we have become rigid, authoritarian, demanding, inflexible, and perfectionistic. We don't know how to listen. We cut people off in conversations and relationships. We don't ask for help. We can't see options. We have little spontaneity or creativity. We experience psychosomatic health problems. We intimidate people by withholding our feelings.

Blindly focused on our pursuit of safety, very often unaware of our emotional self, and yet so frightened and full of shame, we rely on what we know best—control. But the consequences are almost the opposite of what we had hoped for. Our needs do not get met. Our relationships are out of balance. Ultimately, our hyper-vigilance becomes burdensome and exhausting. We don't know how to go about life any differently. In our confusion about what has gone wrong when we've tried so hard to make things right, we succumb to depression and/or resort to unhealthy ways to cope with sadness and pain that often results in addictive behaviors.

While some people don't identify with having tried to be in control of their lives during their growing-up years, they will often speak of how strongly controlling one or both of their parents were, which indicates that the children were victims of control. When these young people grow up they usually react in one of two ways. They may assume a victim position in adulthood, continuing to be in relationship to others who are highly controlling, or they will most likely seek control in every area of life to make up for the lack of personal power they experienced. They are usually at least somewhat conscious of their efforts to have power and mastery over everything in life. They are frequently blatantly angry, though they fail to acknowledge the anger. Typically, their anger is tightly controlled. Very often that anger is a direct response to a parent's controlling relationship.

Adults react to chronic parental control in many ways. For example, people with a food disorder are controlling what does and does not go into their mouth, trying to compensate for the powerlessness they had over the abusive control they experienced. Another example can be seen when one person in a relationship dominates the other, as a result of the anger felt toward the highly controlling parent of the opposite sex. In other words, a woman would dominate her husband in order to act out her anger at her controlling father.

Whether or not we have sought control to make up for the lack of control in our lives, fear and shame are the factors that fuel our need to seek control.

Ways We Try to Control

People demonstrate control in a variety of ways, but the following four postures illustrate particularly common ways people disguise their conscious or unconscious attempts to control.

Sweet Controller—This person is polite, pleasant, and sweet in order to get what he or she wants. We often respond positively to this person, attracted to her seeming innocence or his charming smile, but in reflection we recognize all we know about that person is how sweet he or she appears to be. We realize we have become, often one more time, a part of a "one-up/one-down" relationship and we are in the one-down role. Know, though, that sweetness by itself does not equate to being controlling. It is a lovely virtue. In the context of controlling behavior, however, sweetness is the guise under which one finds control.

Distant Controller—This is the person who is rigidly efficient, emotionally cold, and develops a sense of mastery by paying attention to detail. A person like this is great to have in your life when you need a "detail person" but is difficult to be close to.

Passive Controller—This person is known to many as the Martyr, as is reflected by the words, "I don't care. Do whatever *you* want. *You* are more important than I am. Anyway, it doesn't matter to me." The control attempt lies in the unspoken intent, "But I'll get you in the end!"

Angry Controller—This person is an intimidator who says to the world, "I want what I want, when I want it, and I will get it!"

What all controllers have in common is that they operate from a basis of fear. Their fear has been so great that it has led to their need to protect themselves by staying in control. As a result, they have become disrespectful of other people's needs and boundaries. Ultimately, virtually all controllers will become angry. This is inevitable because they are going through life unable to get their needs met.

As controllers, all that we know about is "all or nothing" and "one or ten." We fail to see that almost nothing in real life is on a "one or ten" basis, but that nearly everything lies in a continuum between the numbers two through nine. So, our experience in life is that we are in total control—or we have just lost it! When we feel our tight hold on control threatened, we scramble to regain control in any way we know.

Yet, if we want to experience recovery, we must let go of some control. Hear the word S-O-M-E. Control is not an "all or nothing" issue.

For those of you in twelve-step programs, what I am saying in no way contradicts the First Step, which refers to the need to surrender, that is, to give up control. What the First Step asks us to do is to give up trying to control what cannot be controlled. This is analogous to the Serenity Prayer:

God grant me the serenity
To accept the things I cannot change,
The courage to change the things I can,
And the wisdom to know the difference.

Willingness to give up control is vital to being willing to engage in the recovery process, but this is not something you learn to do all at once. It is not an all-or-nothing process. As one gives up control it is okay to practice giving up control in those areas that feel psychologically safe. You may begin to practice letting go of control more easily in one setting than another. You may begin by letting go of which store you shop in, which movie you see, or who chooses which route you take on a trip. The more you practice letting go, the easier it will become to begin gradually giving up control in the areas that cause the greatest pain, such as past loss conditions or present self-destructive behaviors.

Control Still Feels Like a Matter of Life and Death

Why are we so afraid of giving up control? We need to know what our belief is before we can challenge it and put it into perspective. For most of us, control still represents what it meant to us as children. If we grew up with chronic loss, then giving up control is often equated with being out of control. When I ask adults what not being in control would have meant to them as children, their answers include a wide range of painful memories such as:

- chaos, confusion;
- being abandoned;
- being left alone;
- not being noticed;
- being called names;
- more anger, fear, sadness;
- getting hit;
- not being valued; or
- dying, death.

Some people feared their or another's physical death. For others, it was emotional death and/or spiritual death, the death of their inner child's spirit. While the above responses are perceptions of adults looking back on childhood, the beliefs have never left. You may be thirty-five years old, but when you experience loss of control it is experienced from the reference of being a child. Someone will be hit, be abandoned, or die.

Yet, as people so often remind me, those beliefs from childhood no longer make sense. *After all*, you may be thinking, *an adult should be able to think things through, so such fears would be childish*. My response is "Who is that speaking?" Where does that internalized "should" message come from? Clearly, it is an echo from a long time ago. What is involved here is the emotional vulnerability a person carries from childhood.

We aren't conscious of these fears—these are internalized fears imprinted deep within our emotional beings that we have never been able to address. Now is the time to do so. We need to explore what control has meant and put it into its proper perspective.

Because the whole notion of control is so important, it may help you to take time to focus on what control symbolizes for you.

�"" ***Sit back in*** a comfortable seat and relax. Breathe deeply. Uncross
your legs and arms. Gently close your eyes and reflect back in
time to your growing-up years.

Recognizing how you exerted control externally or internally, finish
this sentence.

Giving up control in my family would have meant _____.
Giving up control in my family would have meant _____.
Giving up control in my family would have meant _____.
Giving up control in my family would have meant _____.
Giving up control in my family would have meant _____.

If you have difficulty with this exercise, another way to benefit from it
is to describe the controlling behavior. (Remember, controlling behavior was
developed to protect you, so don't be judgmental.) For example:

Not taking care of my mother would have meant _____.
or
Not doing the grocery shopping would have meant _____.
or
Not holding in my feelings would have meant _____.

Repeating these sentences allows you to access a deeper level of honesty.
Now ask yourself if control means the same thing to you today.

As much as we become aware of the frightening connotation that the
issue of control has for us, it is now equally important to remind ourselves
of the positive aspects that come with letting go of some control. It is in
giving up *some* control we genuinely become empowered.

In asking those in recovery to name what they experienced as they let
go of control they responded:

- peace, serenity;
- relaxation;
- ability to listen to others;
- ability to listen to ourselves;
- trust in ourselves;
- lack of fear;

- spontaneity;
- creativity;
- fun, play;
- energy;
- our present feelings; or
- intimacy with self and others.

There are rewards. Here is an example of the four recovery steps applied to the issue of control.

Step One: Describe ways you learned controlling behavior (externally and/or internally) and the feelings you had at that time, whether or not you expressed them. Be willing to feel the pain associated to those times.

Step Two: Identify how that past experience has had an impact on you and how it affects your relationships to others today.

Step Three: Identify specific beliefs you have internalized about the need to be in control, whether or not it is internal or external control. Are these beliefs hurtful or helpful to you today? Identify the ones you want to let go of and those you would like to maintain.

Step Four: Identify the areas in your life where you would like to begin to let go of some control. List them in the order of which is safest (easiest) to the scariest (the more difficult). Begin with the safest (easiest). Share this with a person you trust. Allow them to walk through the process with you.

The chart, "Continuum of Control," offers a useful portrayal of control on a continuum.

Continuum of Control

Control Issues in Rigid, Chaotic, and Healthy Families

1 .... 2 3 4 5 6 7 8 9 10

No Control "1"	Some (S-O-M-E) Control "2–9"	Total Control "10"
Family of Origin:		
Chaotic; extreme disorder. Rigid controls attempted to create some safety.	"Normal." Some order; some disorder. Control not a central family issue.	Rigidity; no apparent disorder. Hidden feelings grow chaotic, threaten to emerge, trigger chaotic events.
Abandonment experiences.	Few, if any, abandonment experiences.	Abandonment experiences.
"All or nothing" thinking.	Life is not experienced as "all or nothing," but as a process.	"All or nothing" thinking.
Survival dependent on following family rules superimposed on chaos to create appearance of order.	Survival or parental approval not dependent on family rules.	Parental approval and protection dependent on following family rules prohibiting natural disorder.
Family rules: Don't talk; Don't trust; Don't feel.	Family behaviors: Talk; Trust; Feel.	Family rules: Don't talk; Don't trust; Don't feel.
Belief: Life is unmanageable	Belief: Some things in life can be managed; some cannot.	Belief: Life is a matter to be managed.
In Adult Life:		
Fear of loss of control of self, feelings.	Loss of control not central fear. Confident and accepting of self and feelings.	Fear of loss of control of self, feelings.
Fear of being abandoned by loved ones.	Not driven by fear of abandonment. Trust in self & others.	Fear of being abandoned by loved ones.
Attempts to control based on past beliefs, feelings, and behaviors or to act out chaos.	Recognition of where you have the power to affect things and where you don't.	Attempts to control based on past beliefs, feelings, and behaviors or reject all control.
External approval sought for beliefs and behaviors.	Internal reference for feelings, behaviors, and beliefs.	External approval sought for beliefs and behaviors.
Poor Inner Adult recovery skills.	Activated Inner Adult skills: validate self, "let go" control, feel feelings, identify needs, set limits and boundaries.	Poor Inner Adult recovery skills.

Feeling Your Feelings

In the process of exploring the issue of control, we quickly become aware of our feelings. And we do have so much to feel about. People will have feelings around every recovery issue. Without exploring and becoming more comfortable with your emotional self you will quickly become stuck in the process. With each feeling there are three areas that need to be looked at:

- Fear of the feeling.
- Identification of the feeling.
- Expression of the feeling.

While many adults are fearful of feelings and incapable of identifying any feelings, other people are very clear about what it is they feel. Usually, though, that is when there is only one dominant emotion. Some people may walk through life and the only feeling they know is their anger, or for another the only feeling they know is their sadness. Others will only know their helplessness.

There are some people who appear to only love life. They are *never* angry, sad, or frightened; they are *always* accepting, loving, and understanding. What is really going on for them is that they have successfully buried these feelings and, on occasion, such feelings burst to the surface in bouts of rage or are manifested in depression.

To make lemonade out of a lemon is great, but to refuse to acknowledge the lemon ever existed is denial—denial of ourselves and our experiences. It is when we can own and accept our feelings, whether they are irritations, fears, sadness, joys, etc., that we are able to love life. To be whole, we want to be able to access a range of feelings. A part of recovery is learning to identify a wide range of feelings and then learn the appropriate expression of those feelings.

Although no parents can be perfect role models, the role modeling we saw in our dysfunctional home was often distorted. Our models for expressing feelings were gleaned from people who denied feelings, contradicted our perception of reality, and generally could not express positive or negative feelings in healthy ways.

We often saw people rage in anger or walk away in silence, succumbing to their fear and helplessness. Many times our parents converted one feeling to another; that is, they became sad when angry and vice versa. They added further confusion when they told us we had nothing to be frightened of when we did. They told us we had no right to be angry but that we should feel grateful.

We wanted so much to love our parents without reservation. Then something would happen. They would act in such hurtful ways that we couldn't totally love them, leaving us confused and feeling guilty. As a result of living with a distorted and twisted expression of feelings, we watched, learned, and repeated the same pattern.

Before you can express certain feelings, you need to face your fears about what might happen if you do. In other words, what are you afraid might happen if, for example, you express dislike for your mother, or if you start to cry because your father left you? Typically, some of those fears are: (1) others won't like me; (2) people are going to be able to see how bad I really am; (3) people will perceive me as weak; (4) they are going to perceive me as vulnerable, and to me that is the same thing as being bad; (5) others will tell me that I have no reason for feeling this way; or (6) I will not be in control and that is not okay.

These fears were most likely valid at one time in your life. When you expressed an honest emotion, your parents and other caretakers may have responded with some kind of rejection, which felt like abandonment. We need to ask ourselves, "Is that still true today?" Sometimes we never ask and yet we operate on fears that are ten, twenty, or even many more years old. If we express our feelings in the presence of certain people and their response is negative, the question we need to ask ourselves is "Do we want to believe that other person's judgment?" Or do we want to validate ourselves, relying on our own internal judgment and strengthening our core of positive self-regard? For a while we will feel anxious about these choices, so we need to confront these fears early in recovery to allow ourselves to be honest about who we are.

You may also have difficulty expressing feelings because you have difficulty identifying them. If so, you need to go back and work on learning to identify feelings. People from family systems that did not sanction the expression of feelings may honestly have difficulty recognizing that their clenched fists and tightly folded arms are signs of anger.

Early in the process of exploring feelings, it is not uncommon to ask people how they are feeling and hear the reply, "I don't know." Many therapists perceive that response as resistance. However, it is my experience that the person probably doesn't know. This is known as psychic numbness, emotional anesthesia, or frozen feelings.

If you are able to identify your feelings and still not express them, that is often due to the fear of what might happen. In this case, your fear needs to be explored further to find the freedom to use your emotional skills.

To summarize, if you find yourself stuck in the area of feelings, you need to assess the problem to see if it has to do with the (1) fear of feeling, (2) identification of the feeling, or (3) expression of the feeling. Remember, do not confuse doing your grief work with the issue of exploring feelings in general. Identifying obstacles in dealing with your feelings will help you develop the skills to do the grief work. At the same time, it will give you the skills to express your feelings in the present.

Feelings are cues and signals that tell us we have a need. If we pay attention to the feeling, we can learn what it is that we need. For example, if you feel some discomfort and reflect on what you are experiencing, you may identify the feeling to be loneliness. Knowing when you are lonely is important and you can deal with that in the present. But if you do not listen and respectfully respond to the feeling, you may try to compensate with some counterproductive behaviors instead, such as overworking or overeating.

It is also helpful to know how you have become accustomed to compensating for your feelings, because those compensatory behaviors are also cues that tell us what we are feeling and what we need. For instance, to recognize overeating as a cover-up for sadness helps you to identify an opportunity to change your feeling response. Many, many people run from their feelings with certain behaviors. Some people use work, exercise, or shopping to distract themselves. Others use food and alcohol to medicate.

Feelings are also indicators that help us set boundaries that provide safety for us. Expressing our feelings allows us to connect and bond with others. This is what allows us to experience intimacy. Our emotional self is significant and vital to the opportunity to experience meaning in life. Yet, that does not mean recovery is about sharing every feeling we experience. A sign of recovery is the ability to know what you feel when you feel it, to be comfortable with your emotional self, and then to be able to determine whether or not and with whom you share feelings.

Here is an example of the four recovery steps applied to feeling your feelings.

Step One: Identify the feelings you had growing up, then note which feelings were okay to express and which were not. What would happen when you tried to express the more unsafe feelings? What did you fear would happen? What did you then do with the feelings that were not able to be expressed? Share these awarenesses with someone you trust. Be open to feeling the pain associated with remembering these experiences.

Step Two: Describe how those childhood experiences impact you today.

Step Three: Identify specific beliefs you have internalized about feelings in general, and then specific feelings. Are these beliefs hurtful or helpful to you today? Identify the ones you want to let go of and those you would like to maintain.

Step Four: Create a feeling list, which names a variety of feelings. Take time out each day, stop, pull out your list, and ask yourself what you are feeling. Is there someone you can share the feeling(s) with at that time or later? Is there something you can do, such as journal writing or a brief relaxation exercise that can serve as an act of self-care should you be having a vulnerable feeling?

Identifying Your Needs

Learning to identify our feelings accesses our ability to recognize our needs. In families marked by chronic loss, children's needs are not met. Adults don't focus on the children's needs and the children don't or can't, because they are too young and without adequate adult support and nurturance. And, as I've said previously, often the children were kept busy taking care of others. For many of us, this focus on others became a safety net, a part of our identity that has carried over into our adult lives. The payoff is "If I don't focus on me, I won't feel the depth of my helplessness and powerlessness." But, as a result of not knowing our needs, they don't get met. No wonder we are depressed, angry, or confused. "Me? Oh, I don't have any needs. No, I don't need anything." *Needs* is spoken as if it is a foreign or even a vulgar word for many of us.

Taking a look at your needs can be as frightening as the idea of looking at your control issues. You will have to let go of some control before you can actively wrestle with the concept of having needs. You will need a strong sense of what your feelings are because your feelings are cues and signals that are critical to help identify needs. You are going to have to believe more in your own worth and that you deserve to have your needs met.

It is easy for people to get caught up in the semantics of the word "needs." In grade school we were taught we only have five basic needs—air, food, clothing, shelter, and water—and everything else is a "want." This was presented as the basis for physical survival. The life you are now rebuilding is not only about physical existence—it is about going beyond. Our psychological, emotional, social, and spiritual needs are that which give meaning to life.

When needs are attended to, children learn skills that allow them to grow emotionally and psychologically, that allow them to move into adulthood with a sense of belonging, a sense of value, and a sense of competence. Regardless of your original parenting, it is no longer going to be your mother or father who will meet your needs. While your needs may not have been met as a child, you have an opportunity to meet your needs now. A major part of recovery is taking responsibility for meeting your needs.

If your needs include establishing new relationships, it will mean finding people in your adult life today who respond to you in a positive, caring manner. This is about reparenting the child who is still within you.

Because many of us were given strong reinforcement for diminishing and not looking at our needs, we need to confront the concept of selfishness. "Is it okay for my needs to be important? Is it okay for my needs to be more important to me than other people's needs at this particular time?"

Amy, daughter of two alcoholic parents, married to her third alcoholic husband, was in a counseling session. When she was asked, "What do you need?" Amy looked at the therapist, confused. She then looked away as if she had answered the question and was ready to move on. The therapist said, "Amy, you have been taking care of other people all of your life. You took care of your parents, three husbands, and two children. It is time to take care of you. What do you need?" Amy, clearly agitated, looked quickly away as if looking for the door. It was obvious she wanted to change the subject. Once again, the therapist said, "Amy, Amy, what do you need? Not anyone else, but you." This time Amy's eyes opened wide and her body began to jerk; her knees jerked up and down; her head jerked slightly back, as if she were going to convulse. Being frightened, the therapist reached out, grabbing Amy where she was twitching the most, at the knee and shoulder. As she was touching Amy, she very calmly, yet firmly spoke to Amy saying, "Amy, it is over. It is all over. You don't have to take care of anyone else. You only have to take care of you."

The twitching subsided. The therapist purposely pushed the obviously very loaded issue and again asked, "Amy, what do you need?" Quietly, Amy responded, "Need? What do I need? In my forty-four years, when has it ever been safe for me to ask myself what it is I need?"

It had never been safe for Amy to consider her needs. Her priority had always been feeling a sense of responsibility for others who were not taking responsibility for themselves. Now, it would be important for Amy to recognize her own needs as an adult in order for them to be met. But, before she would be able to do that effectively, she would need to take a look at what the issue of having needs had meant her entire life, beginning with her growing-up years.

While many adults don't recognize they have needs, many others compartmentalize their needs, rejecting those needs that would involve others. This is the case when someone operates from the attitude, "I don't need you. I don't need them. I'm doing just fine all by myself." This attitude of rigid self-sufficiency is a determined stance to not be hurt or rejected by another.

Colleen, at age thirty-five, was extremely capable. While she allowed herself to get married, she didn't allow herself any interdependency. "I take responsibility for all of my needs. I always have. I never trusted that I would be heard, so I didn't share my desires, my wants. It wasn't that Gerry wouldn't have been there for me—I just didn't give him a chance. I was so used to not trusting that anyone would be there for me or follow through with their promises, it didn't dawn on me to ask others to be there. After all, I became an expert at taking care of myself."

Unfortunately, this dynamic became a major source of discord in Colleen's marriage. She and Gerry were not able to achieve the intimacy Gerry wanted and he ultimately chose to leave the marriage. Colleen stayed out of any committed relationships for the next twelve years. Looking at her issues of trust, fear of rejection, and fear of asking others to be there for her needs is her focus in recovery today. It is Colleen's hope that she will allow herself the intimacy she deserves.

Identifying Now What You Needed as a Child

To become more skilled at recognizing your needs as an adult, you have to be empathetic to your childhood needs. Because your needs today are often the same as when you were a child, discounting your past needs only serves to detract from believing that you have a right to meet your needs as an adult.

In working with clients, I have found that for adults to identify their unmet needs as children, it is very helpful for them to go through an exercise of writing a letter to their parents. This exercise also leads them to see that those childhood needs are often their needs today. This letter will never be mailed, read to, or given to that parent. The purpose is not to retaliate, blame, or hurt the parent. The purpose is to facilitate the grief process and identify needs.

Here is an example. It is a letter written by a thirty-three-year-old woman.

Dear Dad,

I want to thank you for some things when I was young. I am glad you told me you loved me. I believed it. I always liked it when we played.

But Dad, there was so much I needed that I just didn't get. You became so tyrannical, so controlling, and so dishonest. More than anything, I needed you to let me be a kid, to let me make mistakes. I lived in fear of not being perfect for you. By being perfect in your image, I gave up my childhood. I needed to play, Dad. I needed to be me and not just a part of your self-image.

I needed you to be nicer to Mom. You never remembered her birthday or bought her a Christmas present. Because you drank, she was always at work. I needed to know her better.

As a teenager, I hated the fact I was so fearful of you. I was scared, terrified all the time. I hated how I felt sexually. I felt so dirty because of your attitude about boys and me. I always felt ashamed. The funny part, Dad, is I wasn't sexually active.

I needed to eat dinner as a family. We ate anywhere from 7:30 at night until 11:30. There was nothing ever pleasant about dinner. You didn't even eat half the time.

You know what, Dad—I still need you.

This letter elicits many powerful feelings. This is the kind of letter that helps to move you through the grief process and at the same time helps you become empathetic to your own plight as a child. It also allows you to see how your childhood needs are often carried into adulthood.

In the above letter, this woman identified her childhood needs as:

1. I needed to be a kid.
2. I needed to play.
3. I needed to make mistakes.
4. I needed to be me, not you.
5. I needed to know Mom better.
6. I needed to feel comfortable with my sexuality.
7. I needed healthy rituals.
8. I needed you, Dad.

By identifying these childhood needs, the writer identifies her present-day needs. These aren't needs that her parent will meet today, but they are still present-day needs, regardless of age. An exercise like this says:

1. I need to play, to discover my spontaneity, frivolity, creativity.
2. I need to feel I am of value even though I make mistakes.
3. I need to discover who I am separate from my father's needs of me.
4. I need to know my mother better.

5. I need to feel comfortable with my sexuality.
6. I need healthy rituals.
7. I need my father.

This woman at thirty-three, or at any age, can still work on these needs. Of course, her parents may not be available or accessible, but owning the need is the first step to coming to terms with it.

> ❧ *Take time to* write a similar letter. Choose a person from whom you have experienced loss. After the salutation (Dear _____,), begin by thanking that person for what he or she has given you. Then tell the person what it was you needed that you didn't get. When you get ready to write, with pencil in hand, just begin—don't try to plan or think ahead about what you want to say. Don't be preoccupied with writing form or style. What you say is what is important here, not how well you write.

When you have completed your letter, read it aloud (not to the directed person). There is usually as much power and value in the reading as there is in the writing. This process brings relief as stored feelings are identified and released.

After reading your letter and having time to be with your feelings, go back to your letter and circle the needs you have expressed. The needs you identified in your childhood will give you a focus and direction for needs you can still attend to today.

Recognizing needs as normal and human allows us to be more open to valuing our needs. If you have difficulty focusing on yourself, if you also feel empty, depressed, possibly victimized or angry, repeatedly ask yourself: What do I need? What do I want? What do I need? What do I want?

As you let go of control and feel your feelings, your needs will become more evident. As you continue to practice self-validation you will have a stronger belief that you deserve to have those needs met.

It is in knowing what your needs are that they are most apt to be met. Here is an example of the four recovery steps applied to identifying your needs.

Step One: Create a list of needs you had growing up. Most of them will be the needs any child would have. Don't be shy; remember, you were a child. Then describe how those needs were or were not met by your parents or primary caregivers. On a scale from one to ten, one being the least, ten being the most, rate how that need was met by the different caregivers. Be willing to feel the feelings associated with those experiences.

Step Two: Describe how those childhood experiences have an impact on you today.

Step Three: Identify specific beliefs you have internalized about having needs and having your needs met. Are these beliefs hurtful or helpful to you today? Identify the ones you want to let go of and those you would like to maintain.

Step Four: Identify needs you have today. Don't be surprised that they aren't exactly the needs you had as a child. Then identify a way you can go about getting each of those needs met. Begin with those that are the easiest and least scary. Develop a strategy that is realistic.

Setting Limits and Boundaries

Beginning to meet your needs leads you to the next recovery skill, which is setting limits and boundaries. Being raised in troubled families meant that your boundaries as children were not respected, often not even recognized. Or you may have lived with rigid, walled boundaries, offering no opportunity for any emotional or spiritual connection. Unhealthy boundaries create confusion about who is responsible for what, adding to more distortion about guilt and shame. As a result of living with chronic boundary violation/distortion, you are often either not skilled in setting boundaries or you are disrespectful and intrusive of others' boundaries.

A boundary is a limit or edge that defines you as separate from others—a separate human being, not someone else's possession. For each of us, our skin marks the limit of our physical self. We have other boundaries as well. We have limits to what is psychologically and physically safe. We have emotional, spiritual, sexual, relationship, and intellectual boundaries.

Emotional boundaries define the self, our ideas, feelings and values. We set emotional boundaries by choosing how we let people treat us. Our spiritual development comes from our inner self. Only we know the spiritual path for ourselves. We have sexual boundaries, limits on what is safe and appropriate sexual behavior. We have a choice about whom we interact with sexually and the extent of that interaction. We have relationship boundaries. The roles we play define the limits of appropriate interaction with others. Our intellectual boundaries offer us the opportunity to enjoy learning and teaching. They allow us to be curious and inspired.

Because we were raised with unhealthy boundaries, we often normalize hurtful behavior and can't recognize boundary distortion. The following are various types of boundary violation.

Emotional

Feelings denied.
Told what we can and cannot feel.
Being raged at.
Being criticized.
Being belittled.
Lack of expectations.
Being terrorized.

Spiritual

Going against personal values or rights to please others.
Taught to believe in a hurtful Higher Power.
No spiritual guidance.
No sense of prayer or gratitude.

Sexual

Being sexual for partner, not self.
Lack of sexual information during puberty.
Given misinformation about our bodies, our development.
Exposure to pornography.

Sexualized comments.

All forms of sexual abuse.

Relationship

Falling in love with anyone who reaches out.

Allowing someone to take as much as he or she can from you.

Letting others define your reality.

Believing others can anticipate your needs.

Intellectual

Denied information.

Not allowed to make mistakes.

Not encouraged to question.

Being called stupid.

Encouraged to follow a parent's dream rather than your own.

Physical

Accepting touch you do not want.

Not taught appropriate hygiene.

Violence, pushing, shoving, kicking, pinching, excessive tickling.

Hitting.

Touch deprivation.

Boundaries are the mechanisms that bring safety into our lives by establishing healthy control. Boundaries are statements about what we will and will not do. Boundaries act as limits for what others can and cannot do to us. By setting boundaries for ourselves, we are exercising our inherent power to declare that we are autonomous individuals in our own right, not possessions or extensions of anyone else.

As a child, you had little power to determine your interactions with the world. You had no way to defend against boundary invasions. Yet, being invaded—used, abused, or violated—you believed you had no personal worth, having been treated as an object or possession, not a person. You may have believed you were bad or weak because you couldn't stand up for yourself. Today, as an adult, you can develop and strengthen boundaries, giving you a source of inner strength.

Before you can establish healthy boundaries, it is helpful to the process to identify boundary violations in your life.

✤ *Think about significant* people in your growing-up years and reflect on the six areas of boundaries with each person. Note the healthy boundaries and unhealthy boundaries that were experienced.

✤ *Repeat this same* exercise with the significant people in your life today.

Once identified, you are in a better position to redefine them for a healthier self.

Healthy boundaries are flexible enough that we can choose what to let in and what to keep out. We cannot maintain boundaries without the ability to know our feelings. Feelings are our signals to comfort, safety, discomfort, danger.

We want to have boundaries that are flexible but with limits; they move appropriately in response to situations—out for strangers, in for those we are intimate with. They should be distinct enough to preserve our individual self, yet open to new ideas. They are firm to maintain values and priorities, open to communicate our priorities. Boundaries tell us that certain behaviors are inappropriate in the context of certain relationships. A healthy boundary protects without isolating, contains without imprisoning.

Our ability to protect ourselves psychologically and physically is related to the strength of our boundaries. Boundaries bring order to our lives. As we strengthen our boundaries we gain a clearer sense of ourselves and our relationship with others. They empower us to determine how we'll be treated by others.

Establishing healthy boundaries is vital to recovery, to getting needs met, to developing a sense of self. All of this leads to being strong enough to be able to separate yourself from past shameful messages and behaviors—and to no longer internalize shame.

Developing boundaries is knowing your physical and psychological comfort zone—a safety zone—knowing what you like and don't like. It is having a sense of your own self separate from others. It is a part of defining who you are.

In recovery you need to ask yourself what it is you want. What do you need? What do you desire? One establishes boundaries that allow those wants to happen. Limit setting is the skill that allows one to maintain boundaries. In order to protect boundaries, in order for them to remain intact and useful, you need to know your feelings. Feelings are cues and signals to whether those boundaries are being respected. As well, one must believe their needs are important to be able to define boundaries.

Fear of rejection, the need for approval, and fear of anger are major stumbling blocks to defining boundaries and a willingness to set limits. If you believe you have done the work you need to do to be better skilled in establishing boundaries, but are nonetheless stuck, go back and address these three stumbling blocks.

The skills to be able to set limits and establish boundaries take you to another issue and that is the ability to say *no* and *yes*. By establishing boundaries and setting limits, you begin to use the words *no* and *yes* with freedom. For so many of us, it was not safe to say *no* as a child. Without the freedom to say *no, yes* was said with tremendous fear and helplessness or out of a desperate need for approval and love. Others of us grew up in families where *no* meant *yes* and today we cannot hear when people say *no*.

There is often pain and confusion around how *no* and *yes* were offered in troubled families. That pain needs to be acknowledged. As with the other foundation issues, you will need to apply the four steps to *no* and *yes* in your life.

A part of recovery will mean talking about the many times you couldn't say *no* but wanted to (all the times you said *yes* out of fear), and the anger and the pain that goes with that. You need to acknowledge the times you heard *yes* when you needed to hear *no*. In recovery you will recognize that *no* can be a word that acts as a friend to protect you. It offers you choice. In doing so it will allow you to be more sensitive to others' boundaries. We all have the power and right to say *no* and *yes*. It is my hope that *yes* is a right that is offered freely rather than out of fear or the need for approval, and that when you say *no* you are actually saying *yes* to yourself.

Here is an example of the four recovery steps applied to setting limits and establishing boundaries.

Step One: Describe both the healthy and unhealthy boundaries you experienced in your growing-up years. Be willing to feel the pain associated to those experiences.

Step Two: Describe how those childhood experiences have an impact on you today.

Step Three: Identify specific beliefs you have internalized about setting limits and establishing boundaries. Are these beliefs hurtful or helpful to you today? Identify the ones you want to let go of and those you would like to maintain.

Step Four: Name specific boundaries that you would like to either strengthen or lessen. List them in the order of which is the most safe (easiest) to the more difficult ones. Begin with those that are safest. Congratulate yourself with each accomplishment!

Creating a Core of Strength with the Recovery Skills

The core recovery skills—validation, giving up control, feeling feelings, identifying needs, setting limits, and establishing boundaries—are the skills that will allow you to move forward with growing confidence. They are the skills that will offer you a foundation to go further in recovery and address more complex issues of loss, abandonment, and shame. You will be developing a true inner sense of self that will allow you to discover new choices and bring meaning into life. You will no longer just be a reactor; instead you will act on your own beliefs and decisions. You will no longer be propelled by fear or shame, but you will have a more solid belief in what you value, what you want, and a much more gracious, supportive, and forgiving attitude toward yourself.

Life will no longer be viewed through a lens of fear or doubt. You will rightfully expect more from life and feel hopeful. The foundation has been laid for you to continue addressing those areas important to you. There are two cautions that may be helpful to stay aware of:

I want recovery, but I'd like the process to be pain free.

I want recovery, but I would prefer to do it by myself.

We would all like to avoid going through emotional pain—I know I certainly would. But we need to own and feel that which has been harbored in our body and soul so we can set it free. And, as I will soon discuss, our *fear* of feelings is often more powerful than anything that actually occurs when we feel. Know that you never again have to walk through the pain as a child and that you never again have to walk through the pain alone.

While you would like to reach recovery alone, recognize that you have lived a life of isolation. So, wanting to go through this process alone often reflects the rigid self-reliance you learned, as well as not having learned to trust. You deserve to have help by allowing others to be a part of your process. There are many who will understand your emotional struggles and pain. Whether you choose to begin your recovery with a therapist, a twelve-step group, or in treatment, there are literally millions of others who understand your resistances because they have struggled, too.

The awarenesses that have brought you to your turning point are much like a sailboat changing course. The boat simply "comes about," turns to a new direction, and the wind refills the sails. As you change course, the steps you now know, along with the skills you are learning, will harness or guide the power of the wind to help you move along your newly chosen way.

↳ You deserve to begin rebuilding your life in a new direction.

↳ Learning to love yourself does not mean you love others less. Instead, it frees you to love them more.

Changing Course

From a Childhood of Chronic Loss and an Adapted Adult Lifestyle

Abandonment experiences:
  Conditional love
  Boundaries violated

Family of origin conditions:
  Denial
    Rigid and /or chaotic
    Isolation /disconnection
  Shame

Family of origin rules:
  Don't talk
  Don't trust
  Don't feel

Feelings as a child:
  Afraid, ashamed
  Helpless, powerless
  Angry, guilty
  Lonely, sad

Personality characteristics as an adult:
  Dogmatic
  Rigid
  Controlling
  Dependent

Feelings as an adult:
  Isolated, lonely
  Unlovable, unworthy
  Shameful, angry, sad

The Four Steps to Freedom

1. Explore past losses
2. Connect the past to the present
3. Challenge internalized beliefs
4. Learn new skills

Grieving Past Feelings and Processing Present Feelings

1. Embrace the feeling
2. Identify the source
3. Grieve the pain
4. Express the feeling here and now

Core Recovery Skills

1. Validate self
2. Let go of some control
3. Feel feelings
4. Identify needs
5. Set limits and boundaries

The Recovery Process

Core Recovery Issues	To a Recovering Adult Lifestyle
Pain: 　Abandonment: loss events 　Abandonment: loss conditions 　Shame 　Control 　Fear *Pain responses:* 　Victim stance 　Rage 　Depression 　Addiction 　Compulsion 　Perfectionism 　Procrastination	*Loss acknowledged, not abandoned* 　Unconditional love 　Boundaries maintained *Adult/Family conditions:* 　Reality, no denial 　Flexibility 　Interdependence, connection 　Shame-free *Adult/Family rules:* 　Okay to talk 　Okay to trust 　Okay to feel *Personality characteristics as an adult:* 　Open 　Flexible 　Noncontrolling 　Interdependent *Feelings as an adult:* 　Connected to others 　Loved, worthy 　Shame-free, serenity

Chapter Five

The House We Lived In

No More Roles, No More Secrets

"What if we thought of the family less as the determining influence by which we are formed and more the raw material from which you make a life."

—Thomas Moore

"Stand tall in the face of truth. Trust in your perceptions. Give voice to your reality."

—Claudia Black

A family is like a house with many rooms. Picture the family you grew up in as one room in the framework of this very large house. The family you have now, as an adult, is the central living area—in fact, the "family room." Each of the other, different rooms of the house represent the previous generations of families and newly created ones, all of which are connected directly or indirectly. Through the doors to those rooms pass family secrets, family stories, and beliefs about what is and isn't true, and what a person should and shouldn't do.

Family Secrets

As we attend to our childhood issues, as we lessen our denial, we discover our true selves, and we may uncover family secrets. This is very frightening to family members who have spent years protecting themselves, and possibly others, from the pain of the truth. Recovery means letting go of the secrets.

Secrets are handed down from one generation to another. Secrets are pieces of information that are withheld from others often out of shame, and many times with the intent to protect someone, be it yourself or another.

After his mother died, Kevin discovered a secret she had kept. Her parents had been from Austria, not Switzerland, as he had been told. Because of fear of religious persecution, they had changed their name and even the facts about who they were and where they had been born.

In Megan's case, her mother consciously chose not to tell her that she might pass on a physically disabling terminal illness to any male children. Afraid that no man would want to marry Megan, her mother thought if her daughter never knew, she would not be limited in her marriage options. In time, Megan had many suitors and did marry, but she also bore a child who died young from this transgenerational illness. The mother's concerns were sincere and out of love, but in trying to protect her daughter as she did, she denied Megan the chance to make important decisions for herself.

As is often the case, the intent of the secret was to protect. While both Kevin and Megan understood their parents' concerns, Kevin was not able to share a piece of history and this created pain for him. He didn't have the opportunity to assist in lessening his mother's shame as he would have liked. He lost an opportunity for a significant intimate passage. As a result of her lack of information, Megan would experience the consequences of a decision her parents made for her, a decision that undermined the possibility of choice.

The Power of Secrets

Secrets are powerful because they can control you. Very often, the problem with a secret is not the content of the secret itself, but what you must do to keep the secret information out of sight. In a family, it is the proverbial skeleton in the closet and everyone in the family is held responsible to remain on guard in case someone outside the family gets too near the closet door.

Whether secrets are passed down unbeknown to others or people actively collude to hide the information, it is fair to say that as a young child you had no choice in the matter; you were more or less coerced to keep the family secret. As an adult, you are now enforcing that secrecy on yourself. You may not be aware of it but you are the one making the choice to keep certain information away from prying eyes. The secret is just that—only information—and the choice is yours to tell it, to admit it, or to keep it hidden.

By admitting the reality of what is, you deflate the power of the secret. You can't drink away, exercise away, eat away, work away, or by any other effort rationalize away the power of the secret. The only way is to end denial, to admit, to open the closet door—that is the only way to get free.

⇄ The awareness that now you can choose to be free from the secret is a turning point.

Living in the Shadow

Being raised in a shame-based family means being raised in a family where there is a pervasive need to deny that family secrets exist. The content of the secrets may be especially fearful, seem especially awful, or the adult secret-keepers may be particularly rigid about the need to keep up appearances. Whatever the reason, all family life goes on as if under a dark cloud because denial blocks the light of truth and shame grows rampant in the shadow.

Kevin's and Megan's mothers were the self-appointed, lonely guardians of the family secret, but some of us were raised in families where secrets were blatantly shared. In Lawrence's case, he reflects, "My dad had to go to the psychiatric hospital periodically. He was manic depressive. We know that now, but we didn't know it when I was a child. Each time he went, all of us kids were told not to tell anyone. If someone asked where he had gone, we were supposed to say he had to go back East to see a sick relative." Cyndy remembers that "my older sister became pregnant twice, and each time we made up a lie for where she went for the last few months of her pregnancy. As soon as the lie was created, we were never to talk about her being 'gone' again."

These are secrets the family members actively collude in. Yet, many of us live with secrets we don't even recognize. We may have lived with the secrecy of alcoholism without knowing it for what it was. Robin said, "I thought my dad was just crazy. He was forever a different personality. I knew he drank a lot, but so did lots of other people we knew. I didn't know he was addicted."

When we keep secrets we become adept at rationalizing and tolerating inappropriate behavior. As Sean said, "I thought I came from a normal family. But it was only after three years of being sober that I started to take a look at most things in my life. I began to see that it's not normal for parents to make their children drink from a toilet because they are caught playing in it. It is not normal for parents to create 'beating circles' with their children to discover which one did something wrong."

In circumstances like Sean's, there was no overt attempt to maintain secrets. Instead, there was a climate of secrecy about what occurred within the family. Pain was inflicted on purpose, but the children knew nothing different; the family was their only experience. Common to so many shame-based families is the phenomenon of not knowing what "normal" is because everyone learns to tolerate inappropriate behavior. With the Don't Talk rule strongly intact and no other role models due to the family's isolation, all the family members are subject to ongoing hurtful behavior.

When we experience something in life that we don't have the language for, we literally can't talk about it, so the experience remains a secret. For example, some children don't identify their being abused because they are taught that physical abuse means being punched or slapped. They don't recognize that having their hair pulled is abusive. They don't recognize that being slammed up against the wall is abuse. Also, they may believe a certain behavior has to happen every day, so when it only happens once a month, they rationalize it and it remains a secret.

Any time we do not have support within the family for our feelings, we learn to deny the pain and to create defenses that protect our vulnerable self. In time, we normalize painful experiences. "It only happened once." Or, "He didn't mean it." There is a need to deny and to protect ourselves when we don't have the external protection from other family members that we need in order to survive. When that happens, we end up keeping secrets and not even recognizing the secrets are there.

For some people the word *secret* implies an accompanying negative judgment. They believe that if the secret were known, they would be judged as damaged goods, as "less than," or "not as good as" others. Naturally, it is difficult for people with this belief to open up and admit their reality.

How can you tell if you are living with a secret? One way is to ask yourself, "Is there something about me or about my family that causes me to fear, if the truth were known to others? Would I be rejected as their lover, friend, or employee?" Another way of asking is, "Is there something I cannot tell anyone because I am afraid of a negative reaction?" When you feel an implied threat associated with divulging some certain knowledge, this is information that restricts your life.

❖ *Name the secrets* that have been held in the family in which you were raised.

The Origins of Secrets

What secrets did you grow up with? Were these secrets you were aware of at the time or secrets you suspected and then confirmed later?

Secrets are often about embarrassing illnesses or problems with the law, such as being convicted of a crime or being in prison. Other problems occur in situations where family members have had extramarital affairs, pregnancies outside of marriage, abortions, addictions, or are involved in physical or sexual abuse.

What secrets do you have as an individual? There may even be some things only you know. Randall said he stole as a child and even now steals little things from friends and family. As far as he knows, no one knows that. Jeanne said she was raped and no one else ever knew. Many women who have been raped have kept that experience and all of the many associated feelings a secret. Delores kept the knowledge of an unwanted pregnancy and miscarriage from her own husband.

Some of us have secret fears, such as "What if I lose my mind like my mother did?" Other fears might be, "I'm afraid my marriage is about to end" or "I am questioning my sexual orientation."

As we keep our secrets and carry the burden of hiding the information, feelings of guilt often intensify and fear of discovery escalates. Fear causes pain, and too much pain often pushes us into seeking some self-destructive means of temporary pain relief. People keeping the secret of being sexually abused are commonly known to medicate their pain with alcohol, pills, or other drugs. Many people isolate themselves socially so they don't have to spend energy focused on what they "can't say." It is common to see someone in addiction recovery have a relapse when he or she feels extreme guilt for a secret or even from the fear of discovery of a secret.

When we carry secrets, our view of the world is distorted. We are forever in a defensive position with others because we are always on the alert to protect our privacy. Trying to somehow distance ourselves from this "hidden information," we rationalize, distort, and repress the information in a way that blocks us from opportunities for emotional growth and intimacy. Phyllis, for example, didn't want her new boyfriend to get close to her family because she didn't want him to know certain things about them, such as her mother's addiction to pills or her brother's chronic abuse of cocaine. As a result, she would spend energy trying to stay separated from a significant part of her life. By not sharing the history of being sexually abused, Marie maintained a barrier between her partner and herself that directly contributed to the sexual difficulties they were having as a couple.

When we have lived a life of secrecy, after a while it just no longer occurs to us to share with and confide in others. When we haven't talked about something for five, ten, or even thirty years, it doesn't occur to us to talk about it today. We have had years of training in being closed, protective, and secretive. So when things occur in the present that create fear, guilt, or shame, it is even less likely that we would choose to share. And the longer we hold in those old experiences, the more our shame is fueled and the more we act it out.

Out of the Shadows, Out of the Shame

Recovery is living a life free from shame. It is recognizing that you are not your secret; you are not your family secrets. You are a person with myriad experiences, some of them very painful. But, the pain of exposing the secret very, very rarely compares to the pain of keeping the secret. And, once the shameful knowledge is shared, the relief feels like the warmth of the summer sun after a very long, cold winter.

The following are some of the reasons people reveal secrets:

1. **It relieves a burden.** You no longer have to continue to lie to others. The secret has made life more difficult. It is no longer necessary to spend any more energy keeping it. Tony found that he felt great relief when he told his parents, twelve years after the fact, that he was the one, not his brother, who was driving the car when they had the wreck where another passenger was seriously injured.

2. **It allows you to be true to yourself.** It allows you to be honest with yourself. By telling the truth, Tony didn't have to suffer guilt every time he lied about his car wreck. When he could answer, "I was the driver," he could validate himself for having the courage to admit he had made a serious mistake.

3. **It prevents a possible surprise discovery.** Some secrets are shared to lessen the shock or surprise that would be created if a significant other inadvertently found out. In fourteen years of marriage, Michael had not told his wife he had fathered a child sixteen years earlier. After this long time, Michael found tremendous relief believing that, even though it might be painful for his wife to learn he had a daughter and that he had kept the knowledge hidden all these years, it would be better for her to know now. He had decided that was a better option instead of some future day when the daughter might appear on their doorstep.

4. **It enables you to have a more honest relationship with another.** When you share a secret with someone, you are conveying the added message that you trust him or her with something very important to you. You are sharing at a more vulnerable level and that often creates in the other person a reciprocal willingness to be open and vulnerable. The result is that a greater trust develops between the two of you.

5. **It stimulates family change.** When you decide to speak up, other family members are encouraged to make changes in their own lives. By telling your brothers and sisters that your mother has a drinking problem (that all of you have been witness to but have ignored), you are taking the first step in breaking everyone's denial. Potentially, this could result in everyone receiving help, including your mother.

By telling of your sexual abuse, you may set an example that will inspire other family members who have been abused to speak up.

6. **It could be a plea for help.** When the secret you confide still needs to be attended to (for example, if you are drinking too much and not yet in recovery), telling another person is a way for you to begin to move yourself toward getting help. If you were raped, telling someone, even many years later, may be your cry for help that will allow you to process unresolved grief and rage.

Secrets Become Confidences Shared with Safe People

As you create new ways of relating to the people in your family, it will be important for you not to play a part in the secrecy they may still want to maintain. Recovery does not include secrecy. It means speaking your truth. You must end the Don't Talk rule for yourself. However, putting an end to secrecy does not mean that all things are to be shared with all people. Some events are very personal, and you will not want to share them with just anybody. As you choose safe places and safe people to share with, the word *secret* dissipates, and the word *confidence* replaces it.

As you consider with whom you want to share your secrets, you need to examine *why* you want to tell them. Sometimes people share secrets not to help themselves but to hurt others. Some people share a secret for the pure act of revenge. "You have hurt me, so I will hurt you with this! Did you know that Dad isn't your real father?" Any time anyone considers telling some powerful and potentially hurtful information, it is necessary to look at the motivation. You could rationalize that the other person has the right to know. Yes, he or she does. But are you the one to tell the other person? Would it be more helpful to encourage a more appropriate person to share at a more appropriate time?

Not only do we need an understanding of why we are sharing, but also we need to discriminate *with whom* we share confidences. If you picture your family in that multigenerational home, know that you do not need to stand naked in front of your whole family. There is room for privacy. Curtains can be drawn around you or you and certain others. By choosing safe people to share your confidential information with, you have developed an intact, flexible boundary. You choose when the curtain is drawn or closed, or whether or not the window blinds are pulled up or partially opened.

The curtain of confidentiality replaces the rigid, cement-walled boundary of secrecy that blocked out all opportunity to create healthy relationships. In recovery you learn to develop boundaries and to trust your internal cues to know with whom and when to share.

When the whole truth is told about the past because it has been previously discounted or even feared, it can be a real shock to the family system as a whole. As we begin to talk openly about what has happened around those experiences in the past, we may choose to do so gradually.

> ✖ *After reflecting on* whether or not you are maintaining secrets today, note whether or not the secrecy is hurtful to you or others.

> ✖ *With each secret,* identify any fear(s) you have about disclosure. Who would you like to have this information? What has gotten in the way of your telling them? Who might be someone you feel safe sharing this information with?

Telling a secret for the first time is a powerful experience. You may feel great relief and exhilaration. The telling may tap a deep well of grief and pain. It is healthier for you to first share this information with someone you trust and know will be able to listen to what you have to say. Often this is a person who is not affected personally by the information. It may feel safer to share this information with a friend, a partner or spouse, another member of a support or self-help group, a counselor, therapist, or physician. Begin where it is safest.

We benefit by hearing our words expressed out loud, allowing others the opportunity to offer us support and/or validation, either for our experiences and feelings or for what we need to do. The sharing of confidences lessens shame, relieves burdens and, in many cases, heightens intimacy.

> �309 A turning point will come when you can identify a safe way to share the secret.

When we address family secrets, we are also creating new family stories. But first, it is helpful to identify old stories. As you read previously, one of Megan's family stories was that you don't share potentially painful information with the affected person; instead, you try to safeguard his or her options and make decisions for him or her. In her recovery, it is Megan's intent for the family story to be rewritten so her family today supports each other as they face difficult choices.

> ❖ *How would you* like to rewrite your story? Consider again that metaphor comparing your family to a large home with many rooms.

There is a new room that is yours for the making. You can decorate it any way you want; you can fill it with the best of your things. You have choices about whom you invite to come in. You can make decisions about how you act in your own room and in the other rooms that make up your extended family's home. Your own room, your own rules—a somewhat frightening, yet clearly exciting, opportunity.

Identifying Family Roles

Another significant change in the homestead comes with the change of family roles. When you change how you interact with others in your family, you are changing your role.

In the early years of understanding children from alcoholic families, it was extremely helpful for people to identify their own role in the context of their family. The concept of family roles became important because it offered a framework that helped affected families understand what was happening in their lives. This also made possible a language for them to talk about their experiences.

In addition, the newly discovered understanding of family roles offered validation to those who had an ability to "look good" on the outside, but who experienced great pain on the inside. The roles and the resulting restrictions helped people understand why it took so long for their pain to begin to show. Also, this was the first time the addicted family was addressed as a system. The labeling of roles has also been extremely helpful in addressing the problems of dysfunctional families whose issue was something other than addiction, such as mental illness.

By identifying our own role in the context of our families, we are able to recognize many of our strengths and vulnerabilities.

᷍   The awareness of your own role is a turning point.

Roles We Have Played

As we address the ways we have been affected by families and begin to change the ways we relate to others as well as ourselves, we will find ourselves moving from a position of adhering to rigid role(s) to building from the strengths of each of them. Today, there are several versions of family roles, most emanating from the original work of the renowned family therapist Virginia Satir. However, as we look at how we change in our relationships, I will address the roles as I wrote about them in *It Will Never Happen To Me*—the Responsible Child, the Adjuster, the Placater, the Mascot, and the Acting-Out Child.

Virtually everyone has strong survival instincts. As children, many of us needed those instincts to stay alive. When our environment was not a safe place, when it didn't have the structure, the order, or the predictability we needed, we did whatever was necessary to create safety. Those experiences became the basis for our survival roles.

Each role offers intrinsic rewards to the individual person and to the family. Responsible Children, for example, bring order to the family chaos, facilitating for themselves and their siblings a predictable environment. In doing so, they personally feel a sense of greater control and often they experience external rewards. Adjusters play a more passive role, contributing to the family stability by being invisible, not having any expectations or demands, creating an emotional insulator around themselves. The Placaters take care of other family members' emotional needs, attempting to alleviate the family members' pain so they feel greater stability and then are also less aware of their own pain. Placaters are often liked for being so caring. The

Mascot's role is to provide relief from the pain and chaos. They are often appreciated for being distracting and the relief that comes with humor. The Acting-Out Children are attempting to be the voice for the family, saying "HELP!" or "Look at us!"

Looking back, most adults see that they played not just one role, but a combination of roles. The majority of people identify with one predominant role and often operated within the other roles on certain occasions. As an example, a person may identify most strongly with having been an Acting-Out Child, but also has a strong Mascot and Adjuster within him- or herself. Or one may have been both a Placater and the Responsible Child.

For the person exploring his or her own roles, it is most helpful to look at each identified role separately from the others. It is easier to identify the strengths and deficits of each individual role, rather than two or more roles in any combination.

As people move into adulthood, they take with them the identity of their family role(s). A person who had been the Responsible Child will most often continue to demonstrate that role in adult relationships by being a leader and being goal-oriented. Mona, who was the Responsible Child in her family, maintained that position. She worked her way through law school, graduating with honors. By age thirty-one she was in private practice as an attorney. But, she was in private practice because she couldn't work as a team member. She needed to be in charge at all times. She had difficulty listening and was fearful of others who made decisions. By this time her third marriage was in trouble and she had no women friends. These were some of the consequences of strict adherence to her role.

People who identify with being the Adjuster still need someone else to provide structure for them to react. Steve was a man of many hopes and dreams but too frightened to make new decisions. He could adapt to any predicament and found his talent in working in large corporations. When they said jump, he did! Move—he did! Fire so-and-so, he did. He had three managers in three years. While other peers were upset, he thrived on change and unpredictability. Initially, his wife of three years liked that he seemed able to listen and that he was so "flexible," but now she demanded some things from him that were very scary. She wanted him to show conviction and initiative, to express his own thoughts. He was too malleable. In one of his many geographic moves in the short time she was with him, she stayed behind and he moved on to a different city.

The Placater, in adult life, continues to take care of people's emotional needs. Emily, at age thirty-two, was still the family referee. She had passed up two job promotions because, if she left the area, "Who would protect Mom?"

While the strengths of these roles are so clear during the growing-up years, it is in adulthood that the deficits of these roles begin to show. The person who was the Mascot often has difficulty being serious and focused. The Mascot can be tolerated in adulthood if this is more of a minor role for them. If it is major, he will have difficulty with genuine intimacy due to wanting to make light of situations, fearful of being able to be serious, or looking at the truth. In a work setting, he may be well liked but his inability to focus, to know when to set aside his antics is often problematic.

Acting-Out Children are often in trouble with society in their young adulthood; they are thrust into systems, such as hospitals or jails. Either they stay a part of such systems or their role changes as a result of that system's intervention.

Because alcohol and other drugs offer such a pervasive way for the acting-out person to behave, many become addicted. At age forty-six, Patty was still acting out her anger. In spite of having a college degree, her addiction got in the way of working in her field and she supported herself by bartending instead. Known for her belligerent attitude, she challenged nearly anyone who was in an authority position, from the local police officers to her bosses. As a result, few people welcomed her presence and she knew it. While Patty remains angry and addicted, many acting-out people are sober and recovering today.

Not all acting-out people become addicted. Depending on the depth of their anger and challenge of roles and authority, some have managed to redirect the strength of their skills and have mainstreamed into society.

Re-evaluating Our Roles

As much as we strive to create a healthier balance in our lives, we still struggle with what we want to keep and what we want to give up in terms of survivorship. After all, we never know when we may need to call upon those survival skills again. As you work on recovery, you will have the chance to see yourself in the roles you have played, and to identify the strengths

and deficits that have been part of each one. Once you have done this, it
becomes easier to recognize what harmful parts of those roles you need to
let go of and what strengths you want to keep and develop.

Listed below are the strengths and deficits that most often accompany
each of the family roles.

Responsible Child

Strengths	Deficits
• Organized	• Inability to listen
• Leadership skills	• Inability to follow
• Decision-maker	• Inability to play
• Initiator	• Inability to relax
• Perfectionist	• Inflexibility
• Goal-oriented	• Need to be right
• Self-disciplined	• Severe need to be in control
	• High fear of mistakes
	• Lack of spontaneity
	• Inability to ask for input

Adjuster Child

Strengths	Deficits
• Flexibility	• Inability to initiate
• Ability to follow	• Fearful of making decisions
• Easy-going attitude	• Lack of direction
• Not upset by negative situations	• Inability to perceive options, power
• Follows without questioning	

Placater Child

Strengths	Deficits
• Caring	• Inability to receive
• Empathetic	• Inability to focus on oneself
• Good listener	• Readily takes on false guilt
• Sensitive to others	• Strong fear of anger
• Gives well	• High tolerance for inappropriate behavior
• Nice smile	
• Warm	

Mascot Child

Strengths	Deficits
• Perceptive	• Distracting
• Sense of humor	• Immature
• Adaptable	• Takes little seriously
• Able to relieve stress	• Attention seeking
	• Can't focus

Acting-Out Child

Strengths	Deficits
• Close to own feelings	• Inappropriate expression of anger
• Less denial, greater honesty	
• Creative	• Inability to follow direction
• Sense of humor	• Intrusive
• Ability to lead (they just lead in the wrong direction)	• Social problems at young ages such as truancy, high school dropout, addiction, teen pregnancy

   ✂ *In which family* roles do you see yourself? Once you have identified the role(s), create two lists, one noting your strengths and the second noting the deficits of the specific roles.

Beliefs Give Strength to Our Roles

It is easy to see that many of the strengths found in our roles are to be valued. The problem is that they may have been learned in a context of fear, and so we still operate with fear as the basis of those behaviors. Or, they were learned in a vacuum; therefore, we didn't learn the value of the opposite perspective. We may have learned to lead, but not follow. Or, we practiced a strength to the extreme, such as being flexible to the point where we couldn't make a commitment to any one position.

    Individuals' experiences within their families are different due to many variables: birth order, ethnic origin, cultural values, economic circumstances, to give a few examples. These variables come into play when they are the source of our core beliefs. The beliefs we are taught, and those beliefs we pick up on our own, become the reasons our individual strengths become stronger, and eventually a rigidly repeated pattern of behavior, that is, an identifiable role. The behaviors are often fueled by our beliefs.

The following are some examples of beliefs we hold that drive our behavior.

Beliefs of the Responsible Child:
"If I don't do it, no one will."
"If I don't do this, something bad will happen, or things will get worse."

Beliefs of the Adjuster Child:
"If I don't get emotionally involved, I won't get hurt."
"I can't make a difference anyway."
"It is best to not draw attention to yourself."

Beliefs of the Placater Child:
"If I am nice, people will like me."
"If I focus on someone else, the focus won't be on me and that is good."
"If I take care of you, you won't leave me or reject me."

Beliefs of the Mascot Child:
"If I I make people laugh, they will like me."
"If I make people laugh, I won't feel my own pain."
"If I make people laugh, they won't feel their pain."

Beliefs of the Acting-Out Child:
"If I scream loudly enough, someone may notice me."
"Take what you want. No one is going to give you anything."

When you are in a painful family system, each of these positions provides some kind of reward. So, for example, the Responsible Child finds that life is more predictable and stable because he or she has taken charge of so much rather than to live with the chaos. This person garners esteem, as there are often societal rewards for good grades in school, a strong job performance, earning them a pat on the head by parents and community members. The Adjuster is not apt to be singled out for negative attention.

The Adjuster is simply not noticed. The Placater is apt to be complimented and to draw positive attention. The Acting-Out Child is rewarded with attention. (For many children, while negative behavior invites negative attention, that is often experienced as better than no attention.)

Feelings Associated with Our Roles

The family role we have adopted, along with the associated beliefs, affects not only our behavior, but also what we do about our feelings. Of course, we all have feelings, but our response is often in accordance with the beliefs, strengths, and deficits of our role.

Here are some examples of responses to feelings as affected by our roles:

The Responsible Child: "I must stay in control of my feelings."
The Adjuster Child: "Why should I feel? It's better if I don't."
The Placater Child: "I must take care of others' feelings."
The Mascot Child: "I must take the pain away."
The Acting-Out Child: "I am angry about it, whatever it is."

Another way roles restrict our lives is that they dictate the way shame may manifest itself in our adult years.

The Responsible Child shows shame with control, perfectionism, compulsivity.
The Adjuster Child shows shame with procrastination, victimization.
The Placater Child shows shame with victimization, depression, perfectionism.
The Mascot Child shows shame with procrastination, ambivalence, heightened distraction.
The Acting-Out Child shows shame with rage and addictions, procrastination.

While the statements above are subjective generalizations, they describe the reality that many people live.

Who Am I, If I'm Not Who I've Been?

Transformation of Roles from Childhood to Adult Life
Our family roles have become the framework for our behaviors in all aspects of life. Our roles affect choices about careers, partners, friends, family, children, coworkers, and the way we feel about ourselves. These roles have framed our sense of identity. In recovery we ask, "Who am I, if I am not the role I have played all my life?"

"Who am I, if I am not the Placater?"
"Who am I, if I am not the Acting-Out Child?"
"Who am I, if I am not the Responsible Child?"
"Who am I, if I am not the Adjuster?"
"Who am I, if I am not the Mascot?"

You are who you always have been—a good and valuable being. Your inner self remains creative, curious, hungry, wanting. Often expressions from that inner person were ignored, punished, or never developed. You no longer need your role as your survival shield because you no longer need to take a protective stance against shame or fear.

When our worth and our identity are no longer defined by a survival role, we have choices about meeting our own needs and developing in our own ways that we didn't have before. We don't necessarily develop a new personality, but we experience life without the need to defend against pain, and that means we are different in how we interact in the world. At the same time we let go of the shield, we honor that role because it served a wonderful purpose by helping us survive. Then the question arises, "What about the strengths I have received from my role(s)?"

Here are some of the specific questions people have:

"I am a nurse professionally. If I recover from caretaking everybody, does that mean I will have to change careers?"

"Anger is the only feeling I have ever known. Do I have to give it up?"

"My being so responsible and organized has made me a lot of money. I am a very successful businessperson. Will recovery take that away?"

"Flexibility is my name. Will I lose that quality if I look at these issues?"

Recovery does not mean that you are saying goodbye to the strengths of the role. While you want to keep the strengths, you can learn skills that create greater balance in your life. You can develop skills to replace the deficits of the role, and you can learn the skills of the other roles. Part of your new development comes with understanding why you act and react as you do. Another part is practice, revising your beliefs as you explore, questioning them, and gradually risking new behaviors that are congruent with what you really think and feel.

As you attend to the issues that cause you pain or restrict your personal freedom, you begin to develop a more rounded sense of self. You will not need the role to be the source of your worth, your identity. You will be defining yourself from a broader perspective—a perspective of ascertaining your own values. You will be able to listen to your internal cues about what you need. You will have created belief systems that support a way of life you choose, versus a protective stance against shame or fear. And at the same time you can honor that the shield of your role helped you survive and so served a wonderful purpose.

These are the gifts you can maintain or develop:

The Responsible Child

- Maintains leadership skills, ability to organize, takes initiative but lets go of the need to be in control.
- Develops the ability to listen, to follow, to be flexible, to relax.

The Adjuster Child

- Maintains flexibility, ability to be a team player.
- Develops ability to initiate, make decisions, perceive options.

The Placater Child

- Maintains empathy and diplomatic skills.
- Develops ability to care for self, ability to prioritize for self.

The Mascot Child

- Maintains sense of humor.
- Uses own perceptiveness to show compassion.

The Acting-Out Child

- Maintains ability to identify own anger, to speak truth, to lead.
- Develops ability to lead in more positive direction.
- Healthy expression of anger, problem-solving skills.

As we reexamine the roles that have defined our lives, we have to also examine and revise our old beliefs.

Responsible Child **beliefs** transform

> **From:** "If I don't do it, no one will."
> "If I don't do this, something bad will happen or things will get worse."
> "I am not of value unless I am being productive."
>
> **To:** "If I don't do it, someone else will and that is okay."
> "If I don't do it, it will be done differently, and that is okay."
> "I am of value 'being,' not just doing."

Obviously, we hope to get to a place of acceptance where it is really okay for someone else to do those things we would normally take on. We will come to believe we are worthy and of value even when we are not doing all of the performing. It is okay to just "be."

Adjuster Child **beliefs** transform

> **From:** "If I do not get emotionally involved, I won't get hurt."
> "I can't make a difference."
> "It is best to not draw attention to myself."
>
> **To:** "If I don't get emotionally involved, I will never have a meaningful connection."
> "I do make a difference. I am of value and people will value me."

"I deserve attention."

While we seldom seek the "star" role, we come to feel comfortable in our visibility. We can feel a strength we did not allow ourselves to appreciate previously.

Placater Child **beliefs** transform

> **From:** "If I am nice, people will like me."
> "If I focus on someone else, the focus won't be on me."
> "If I take care of you, you won't leave me or reject me."
> **To:** "I am likeable without having to take care of others."
> "It is okay to have the focus. I am deserving."
> "I don't have the power to keep you with me, and if you stay, it is because of who I am, not what I do for you."

Mascot Child **beliefs** transform

> **From:** "If I make people laugh, they will like me."
> "If I make people laugh I will feel no pain."
> "If I make people laugh, they will not feel pain."
> **To:** "I have many attributes that make me likable."
> "Laughter doesn't take the pain away, it masks it."
> "I can tolerate my own pain and others pain."

We learn to take care of ourselves as well as we have of others. We recognize that selfishness is not bad; it is an act of self-care.

Acting-Out Child **beliefs** transform

> **From:** "If I put my face in theirs, they will notice me."
> "Take what you want—no one is going to give you anything."
> "My needs override everyone else's."

To: "I can ask for what I want and listen to the other person at the same time."

"While my needs are important, others' needs are to be acknowledged as well."

"The world is not out to get me. I'm not here alone."

Redirecting all of the energy put into trying to get your needs met by challenging the world will increase self-esteem, establish a connection to others, and create an ongoing, natural high.

Ending Old Roles

Just as recovery is a process, not an event, so is the task of identifying and reevaluating the roles we have played. These roles are as old as our attempts to protect ourselves from pain. The resulting behaviors have become a matter of habit and the beliefs that have fueled them spring up almost automatically. Paradoxically, the roles do not bring us safety or freedom from pain. They restrict our lives in ways we can scarcely recognize and they are the present-day cause of much needless pain. Rethinking our beliefs and reevaluating our behaviors sets us up to relate to our families, partners, children, friends, and to all aspects of our lives, in a much healthier manner.

 � *Identify the benefits* of giving up the rigidity of your predominant role.

The task of recovering our unique selves, as we revise and renew our current ways of being, begins with awareness.

 ↳ The awareness that we have adopted a protective role is a turning point.

 ↳ The awareness that we no longer need that role to survive is a turning point.

Chapter Six

Recovery Is the
Road to Yourself

New Ways of Being,
New Ways of Relating

"Each man's life represents a road toward himself."

—Hermann Hesse

"Recovery is accepting yourself for who you are—no longer waiting for others to define you or approve of you."

—Claudia Black

Many of the Hasidic legendary anecdotes emphasize the uniqueness of every person. "When I get to heaven," said Rabbi Zusya, "they will not ask me 'Why were you not more like Moses?' Instead they will ask, 'Why were you not more like yourself?'"

Recovery is about discovering and becoming your own true self, the essence that is you behind the masks you have put on and the personas you have played while you were trying to please the world around you and keep would-be predators away. What you did—adopting rules and roles to keep yourself a safe distance from others—also created a distance within yourself, a gap between the real you and that unreal, defensive other.

Today you have the opportunity to live with choice rather than to continue a script. Up until now, how you have connected with others has been based on maintaining childhood beliefs and behaviors. When you no longer operate from a basis of fear and shame, you can more easily let go of childhood family rules and roles. When you do, you will find a freedom in relationships not previously experienced.

Relationships, be they with friends, family members or coworkers, have the potential for interdependence rather than dependency or rigid autonomy. You no longer need to go through life in one up/one down relationships. With just your changes, relationships will have a greater opportunity to be based on mutual support because you are engaging from a position of self-responsibility. Even when you interact with others who are not operating from a position of health, you are still acting from a position of positive self-regard and self-care. You are being true to you.

Reconstructing Relationships

As promising as new and renewed relationships can be, leaving the past ways of connecting behind means exiting familiar territory and entering the unknown. When your father raged and you placated him, you could predict that the storm would blow over and calm would return. When you took responsibility for making everyone happy, working until you were exhausted or ill, you could assume that your family would come home that evening so at least you weren't left alone. If you make changes and rock the boat, what will happen?

Uncertainty is one of the things people will face when they make changes. Another is that many people tend to continue in old family roles for fear they will lose face in front of each other. How can the once Responsible Child look to the Adjuster or Mascot for support? And then how will they respond? Will the family now trust the Acting-Out Child to take on adult responsibilities? Will the family reinforce the Placater's guilt or become angry when the Placater doesn't remove family pain? These unknowns can be very frightening to you as you begin your recovery.

When you begin to heal, it is very typical to be enthusiastic about sharing this healing process with others in your family. Yet, very often they are inwardly upset or still in denial, and so they react with a blank look or an even more emphatic verbal response: "What are you talking about?" "I don't know whose parents you are talking about, but they aren't mine!" Or, "How could you be raised in an alcoholic family when I wasn't?" To have significant others blatantly ignore, discount, or deny your reality can be very startling. Even when there is the support of some family members, it can be very surprising how different your experience is compared to your siblings. What we need to recognize is that while we are in a healing process, our family members may have not yet chosen the same path.

Relationships and Expectations

The key for anyone who wants a healthy relationship has to do with expectations. Having relationships with individuals who are not in the growing process can be limiting. If not in their own recovery process, they cannot be as honest, open, nor as nurturing. They may be intrusive and inappropriate in their behavior and expectations. It is crucial, then, for you to adjust your expectations and to recognize and accept the limitations.

You certainly have the right to tell someone else what you need. When you try to get your needs met by someone who is incapable or unwilling, disappointment is sure to follow. When you stop expecting to get what can't or won't be given, the relationship becomes healthier for you.

> ⤷ The turning point in your relationship is the awareness that your growth is not about getting other people to change.

Your loved ones are not necessarily asking or choosing to live their lives differently. It is true that when change occurs, it creates the potential for change among others. The changes they see in us may be what things they desire for themselves. You may be a model that offers them hope. The bottom line is, this recovery process is about you and you creating change for yourself. Everything else that comes is an unexpected gift.

Difficult Family Relationships: Staying Connected with Limitations

The struggle for so many recovering adults is how to interact with members of their childhood family—their parents and siblings. Cultural and family values influence the messages and feelings you received regarding family loyalty and commitment. Typically, we want to stay connected with our families. But, how do you reenter the arena of family relationships and be true to who you are and what you believe? Your efforts may be tentative at first; you will have to learn somewhat from trial and error. Everyone's situation is unique and every individual will need to sort through these issues in a way that is comfortable to them.

It is common to hear adults express loneliness and sadness that their recovery has further alienated them from various members of the family. When a family has not developed healthy alliances or communication patterns, for example, one family member's recovery is often confusing for the non-recovering members.

Being with family members may mean having more superficial interactions—sharing the daily routine without intimacy, recreational interactions, carrying on family rituals (for example, perhaps baptisms, holiday dinners, bar mitzvahs). These traditional occasions may be one way to maintain connection to ones you love. Even superficial contact provides connection. Your choice (remember, you *do* have choices here) may be to choose this level of involvement over no involvement at all.

It is helpful to know why we are engaging with family. Do we feel a sense of loyalty, duty, enjoyment, or love? Again, people differ as to their history and values, which impact decisions about being loyal and dutiful. In spite of family pain, many people still feel love, and many people have found ways to enjoy certain family members. Or, are we still unconsciously seeking validation or approval? It doesn't seem to matter how old we are, we all want to know that our parents value us. When we don't receive validation in our growing-up years, it often becomes an even more urgent, yet usually denied, need. Unfortunately, sick or unhealthy parents are not as apt to offer validation and approval. They are often no more capable of offering that to us today than they were when we were children. In fact, it is more likely they are now seeking that from us.

People differ in their ways of connecting. In Anna's family, she is the only one in recovery. Still, Anna and her codependent mother are able to share weekend holidays now and then. They enjoy sightseeing together, and when visiting in each other's homes they connect through local gossip and conversations about favorite television programs. For many years, Anna would enjoy taking walks through the woods with her alcoholic father. She would time the visits so he was not drunk; she would limit the amount of the time spent together to ensure greater control over their conversation. It was in this setting that she would find a common ground for them to bond, talking about the leaves, the forest animals, and the trees.

Anna's visits with her two sisters are less frequent because their differences are too blatant. There is too much potential for conflict, so their conversations are limited to the tasks of their daily routines. Certainly, Anna would like more intimacy and more authentic sharing, but without greater changes on the part of family she accepts it won't occur.

Nearly all relationships will have certain limitations. By recognizing these limitations we can be realistic in our expectations and far less disappointed by others' attitudes and behaviors. So, in Anna's case, she recognizes and grieves her loss, accepts the reality, and makes her choices. Then she develops other relationships in her life that are more intimate and, in many cases, will provide her with another, healthier bond.

It is common to hear people in recovery refer to others as their family of choice. Maternal or paternal needs are met by older friends and mentors. Sister- and brother-like relationships are developed with peers close to their age. Some adults actually develop a friendship with a person close to their child's age, so they can give to that younger person in ways they had not been able to give to their own child. This relationship option is not intended to negate the parent's earlier experience, but by acknowledging the parent-child loss, there is an opportunity for healing, intimacy, and growth. While you may have lived in the same house and survived a difficult history together, there may be no emotional sense of connection at all between family members. This usually occurs with siblings more than parents, but certainly may be true for both. When a lack of emotional bonding is mutual, family members seldom attempt to connect. Unfortunately, when this is not a mutual feeling, one person is often left feeling rejected and confused. The other person without the sense of connection is often feeling burdened, harassed, and confused, expecting and wanting less in a relationship. It is healthier if you can take responsibility and graciously let the person know you aren't going to make that transition to becoming more connected. This will be a loss but one you can grieve and transcend.

> ✖ *Are you comfortable* with the current relationships with family members? Are there any that would be helpful to create more distance from or more connection with? Describe. If you needed to create a new family of choice, what characteristics would they have that you value?

Maintaining Your Recovery as You Relate to Your Family

The challenge in relationships with people who aren't in recovery is to maintain the integrity of your healing. To take care of yourself it is essential to redefine limits and boundaries. When family members are still in the throes of denial, delusion, frozen feelings, addictions, or compulsions, how much time can you spend with them before the relationship begins to deteriorate? How long before you lose sense of your integrity—in other words, how long before you feel unable to maintain your own boundaries? It may be twenty minutes, two hours, or three days.

To take care of yourself in relationships that are difficult for you, reflect back to what has been the pattern in the past and then plan accordingly. If communication seems to deteriorate after fifteen minutes, limit visits to ten minutes. Setting time limits applies to phone calls as well. You may find the first few minutes are okay, but after that, the old ways go into effect.

In terms of longer visits, you may need to limit the amount of time you spend with parents. Rather than spend one week, stay three days; rather than spend all day, stay three hours. Again, the question is, "What period of time can you be with your parents before you revert to old behaviors?"

Determine for yourself at what points in your family contacts you find yourself not responding as you would like. Use these cues for your limits. Remember that you don't have to decide between "all or nothing," between giving them all you assume they want and never seeing them again. There are almost any number of choices in between these extremes.

Another point to remember is that while we need to own our past role, we do not need to give up the strengths that were part of it. What we give up and what we don't are entirely ours to choose. The important concern is that we no longer make decisions from fear of rejection or need for approval. It is crucial to see that we have a choice.

As you take care of yourself in ongoing relationships with family or friends who tend to operate from the old, hurtful patterns of behavior, you may need to establish boundaries around your conversations. Certain subjects may be taboo because they only lead to old behaviors, for example, "I will not engage in discussion with Mother about my oldest sister because nothing positive comes from it." Is having a subject be taboo the same as having a Don't Talk rule? No. You would be willing to discuss the subject if it could be discussed openly, honestly.

The most important guideline for relationships is to decide what you are willing to do and not do.

- What are you willing to talk about and not talk about? Are there certain conversations you are willing to engage in and others not? Do you need to tell your family ahead of time?
- Are there certain times of the day that are better than others for phone calls or visiting? For example, if your mother is drinking by noon, visit her in the morning. (By the way, do let her know why she doesn't see you in the afternoons.)

Another necessary point is to plan what you need for emotional support prior to your family contact. Let's say you are visiting parents for three days. You may find it helpful, or even necessary, to take daily walks by yourself, to go to a twelve-step meeting, call your sponsor, take your own healthy food, continue to exercise, and/or read meditation books.

Unfortunately, for some people family interactions only result in pain. As a result, some people choose to remove themselves—at least physically—from any and all relationship with their parent(s) and/or other family members. They believe they will feel and be better with distance between family member(s) and themselves. While this may be a healthy decision for some, the all-or-nothing aspect of it is usually not healthy for most.

This is a choice you have and it is your relationship and family history that must be the deciding factors. If you do separate yourself physically from your family, be aware you will still need to take responsibility for your script from that family system. Until grieved and healed, you will be left with your fears, anger, guilts, dysfunctional belief systems, and old defense mechanisms. All too often we take our issues of shame, fear, and powerlessness with us into the other areas of our lives. Remember, the choice to maintain a family relationship is now yours.

Sibling Connections

Siblings within the same family experience life very differently. When Toni was young her family took vacations together, visited amusement parks on weekends, and laughed at her father's antics at the dinner table. By the time her younger sister Dana was seven, their parents had divorced. Vacations and weekend excursions were too expensive for her mother; dinners were often eaten alone with her sister while their mother was still at work. Simply by being older, Toni experienced some stability in her early years that the younger sister would not experience.

There are many variables that affect the development of different personalities in children. Not only are children very different personalities from birth, but also each child enters the family at a different stage in the family's life. One of the major considerations is that each child enters the family at a different place in the progression of the dysfunction that plagues many families.

A clear example of this is when one parent passes from social drinking to problem drinking to becoming an alcoholic. Those children who had access to either the alcoholic or codependent parent in the earlier stages or pre-stages had the opportunity of receiving healthier parenting. They may have received more consistency and predictability, which led to a greater sense of security. They may have received a more consistent show of love, which helped build the child's ability to trust. Typically, the middle and younger children miss the opportunity to experience a healthy (even if sometimes short-lived) family environment. For them, family life is more disruptive and chaotic in their formative years. As a result of birth position in the family, each child has different perceptions and has learned a different style of survival.

Whether a family's life is chaotic as a result of some member's addiction, or a family is rigid and emotionally isolating, the result produces a lack of bonding between siblings. Yet, it is typical that you, as one who is in the process of healing past pain, will want to try to put the pieces of your history together and, in doing so, explore the issue of distance between you and siblings.

Siblings are the witnesses to each other's shame. In each other's presence we mirror back the hurt, disappointment, fear, anger, and shame of our early years. No wonder our contacts are superficial—that helps to avoid remembering our pain. We develop telephone relationships rather than one-to-one contact; we visit only in the company of others. Our conversations are superficial in order to avoid intimacy. We will do whatever is necessary to defend against pain. It is also possible that you grew up so emotionally isolated that you have little on which to base a relationship.

Ideally, people hope to have intimate relationships within the family, but for a great many of us that isn't our reality. Some of us have enough positive connection from childhood that, with effort, healing occurs that fosters intimacy. For others, the estrangement is too great. As a consequence, siblings may connect only through their parents, or they simply don't have contact at all.

While our pain and shame has lessened and we are ready for a more sincere relationship with siblings, they are often not yet at a similar stage of healing. Most likely you, the reader, are the sibling who wants a more intimate relationship. You can offer a sibling information about your experiences within the family and your healing process. As appropriate, you can explain how aspects of his or her life or certain behaviors are related to repressed feelings, hurtful beliefs, or lack of skills not yet learned. But you cannot control whether or not your sibling will listen, hear, and seek his or her own path of healing. In my experience, family members never seem to "do recovery" in our time frame.

Offer feedback as it is appropriate, and then practice the Al-Anon principle of "letting go." Stay focused on your own recovery. Remember that for many people, the business of focusing on others is a distraction from focusing on self.

Sharing Your Pain and Grief with Family Members

In your recovery process, owning what occurred for you in your childhood is necessary. Somewhere you will need to say such things as "I am angry that. . . ," "It hurt when. . . ," and "It wasn't fair that. " This is a natural part of the grief process. It is a part of the process that allows you to own the past and put it behind you. While these statements need to be verbalized, whether or not they are said to family members is an entirely different question.

You need to be "walking the walk" of recovery, not just "talking the talk," before it is appropriate to share with your family what you remember and how you feel. You will need to be comfortable with yourself and your feelings. You also need to have a support system. You will need to have had conversations with others in order to be comfortable with your own truths. You will then be better able to consider what you do or do not want to share with your birth family.

People in recovery can become very verbal, even with strangers, about their histories and feelings. They also listen to others pour their hearts out. As a result, when they share with family they often do so with the zeal experienced in their twelve-step or therapy group, expecting equally reciprocal self-disclosure. You may have more experience trusting the process of honesty than they do. Be realistic in your expectations.

I suggest that you never share newly discovered intimate thoughts with family without having shared them first with someone who is a part of your recovery process. There is much power in saying things for the very first time—we first need to listen to ourselves.

Beth, who has been in therapy for six months, has an opportunity to visit her practicing alcoholic father. She tells her therapist, "I'm seeing my father and I want to tell him about me." When asked what that means, she exclaims, "I want to tell him how angry I am!" Beth has not seen her father in seven years. Their adult visits have been superficial at best. A Christmas card from Beth to her dad in recent years has been her only form of communication. For Beth to share the depth and intensity of her anger after six months of therapy most likely will not be productive. Beth is discovering her anger for the first time in thirty-three years. She is speaking the words for the first time. She needs to know more about herself and her anger. To develop a line of communication with her dad, she needs to determine what part of her anger and how much of her anger she wants to share. She needs to sort out expectations and have a support system more ingrained in her life.

We also feel a sense of urgency that is not always warranted. Nick, twenty-two, who has been in therapy for seven weeks, says, "I need to fly home and see my mom and tell her about all my new thoughts and my feelings about our family." Knowing Nick was planning to see his mother in three months at Christmas, I questioned the urgent need to fly home sooner. Nick responded with, "Well, she could be dead by Christmas." Assuming I missed an important fact regarding his mother being either terminally ill or very old, I inquired, wherein he told me, "No, she's not sick, she's just older. She is forty-six and what if something happens to her by Christmas?" Clearly Nick was reacting to the fear that should his mother die before he was able to see her, he would forever have unfinished business with her. Realistically, Nick's mother is not at high risk of imminent death. Nick was so new in his recovery that he would benefit by more time in therapy before he shared so intimately with his mother.

The following questions are suggested as guidelines to help you explore how much of your feelings and awareness you want to share. As you consider talking to parents and/or siblings, think of what you would say to each of them separately. What you share with one may be very different from another.

QUESTION 1. *What do you want to say?*

Begin this process by thinking about what you want to say, and then understand that you need not say everything. Do you want to tell this person that you are in a healing process related to childhood pain? Do you want to describe the process of healing? Do you want to share specific feelings and thoughts you have had about your life? There is a tendency to think in absolutes—"I need to tell them everything!" Instead, ask "what part?" or "how much of?" In other words, what part of your childhood pain do you want to share? How much of what is discussed in therapy do you want to share?

QUESTION 2. *Why do you want to tell him or her that?*

Examine your motivation for telling something. Sharing demands great honesty on your part. Your feelings and thoughts need to be expressed by saying them aloud, but whether or not you speak directly to the people who are the source of the pain is another question. Will you feel better for having said it? Will it possibly clarify matters for you? Are you saying it to hurt them? Are you telling them things to seek their approval for what you are now doing? Know your motivation. If you aren't sure, wait until you have greater clarity.

QUESTION 3. *What do you hope/expect will happen?*

So many times I've heard people respond with "nothing" in answer to that question. That cannot be the underlying answer because you must have some expectation or your need to talk wouldn't exist. Expectations are usually more realistic when we try to picture very specifically what another's response will be, for example, "I expect my mother to sit as I talk to her." "I expect my father to listen." Sometimes people aren't aware that there is a hope and an expectation until it isn't met. Many hope for an "I love you," or an "I'm sorry." Those responses are possible but not necessarily realistic.

QUESTION 4. *How realistic is that hope/expectation?*

Keep your expectations and hopes low. Most adults have never experienced their family being involved in a recovery process. Family members who are not in recovery most likely will maintain their position of guilt, hurt, or anger. They very likely will repeat their old behavior of ignoring you, blaming, crying, or giving you only a token acknowledgment.

A family member whose life has been changed by his or her own recovery process may be able to hear you today. Still, be realistic. He or she will feel hurt. To expect that family member to not feel hurt is unrealistic. The intensity of his or her response is related to the circumstances in which and how you present the information as well as his or her own emotional and mental health. This does not mean that you should not share. It is simply a fact that you need to be prepared should you share your experiences. It may very well be of greater value for you to share with your family member and allow him or her to feel his or her own pain than for you not to share at all with him or her.

Many people have shared with both recovering and non-recovering family members and have felt relief and validation for the experience. Many have also received the long sought "I love you" or "I'm sorry." The more you think about the situation, are clear about what you want to say, consider the timing, and clarify your expectations to be realistic, the more positive the outcome.

> ❖ *If you are* considering sharing your experiences with a family member, write your responses to the above four questions. Often when we write we are more honest than when we keep our thoughts in our head.

Confrontation as a Part of Sharing

Sharing and confronting are all a part of the same continuum. When people think of confronting someone, they usually think of sharing what that person did that was hurtful. Implicit in this question is, how important is it to one's personal mental health to present specific information about the pain you have experienced to the person who is most directly responsible?

There are many advantages to confrontation. Here are some of the most important ones.

1. Confronting is a way to resolve or bring closure to the relationship or a part of the relationship that plagues you. Bringing closure is important because unresolved relationships will continue to bother you until you get things out in the open and deal with them. Internal conflict over how and if you should confront can cause you to have continual imaginary conversations with the person(s), obsessing about how they would react. Obsessing resolves nothing.

2. Confronting provides an opportunity to set the record straight or to communicate what you need. Confronting those who have hurt

you not only gives them another chance but presents you with the
opportunity to resolve an important issue.

3. If you don't have a confrontation with those who have hurt you, you
    will tend to have inappropriate confrontations with others instead.

4. Confronting those who have hurt you enables you to take back
    your power, proving to yourself that you are no longer going to
    allow anyone to frighten or control you.

5. Confronting those who have caused you damage and pain can help
    to assure that you will not continue to be victimized. When you
    confront you break the cycle of victimization.

6. Confronting is a way of breaking through the denial.

Advantages and Disadvantages of Confronting

Speaking the truth out loud is vital, but whether you confront face-to-face
is another question. This is usually the more difficult dilemma for people.
Not knowing your circumstances makes it difficult for any writer to advise.
The following advantages and disadvantages to direct and symbolic forms
of confrontation may be helpful to you.

The advantages of sharing face-to-face are:

1. You see the person's reactions to what you are saying. This helps you
    to discover how the person really feels about what you are saying,
    about what occurred, about you.

2. It is harder for the other person to ignore what you are saying.

3. It offers opportunity to talk it out at length.

Disadvantages to a face-to-face discussion are:

1. The person you are confronting may resort to the very behaviors
    that were once hurtful to you (for example, verbal abuse, physical
    abuse, condemnation, mockery, prayer vigil), causing you to feel
    confused or frightened.

2. You may not want to know the other person's response. You may
    just want to say your piece without hearing a reaction.

3. The other person's response may confuse or distract you, and you
    may end up saying things you really don't mean.

4. You may find the other person is too busy thinking up a defense to actually hear what you have to say.

↪ You are not a coward if you choose not to confront face-to-face.

Less risky, yet still direct forms of confrontation are using the telephone or sending a letter, text, or email. These have some of the advantages stated but without the risks.

Indirect/symbolic ways of confronting are through the use of therapy techniques such as gestalt, role play, psychodrama, letter writing (letters that are not sent, given to, or read to the person).

Advantages to these indirect /symbolic methods are:
1. You are free to say what you need without fearing the person's reaction.
2. You can maintain the safety of distance and still gain closure in the relationship.

Disadvantages to these methods are:
1. You may feel as if you missed out on having the chance to confront directly.
2. You may wonder what it would have felt like to speak your mind. If you do not choose to confront directly, it does not exclude the possibility of doing the direct confronting at another time.

If you choose a more direct method, problem-solve in advance. Plan the place, the setting, and what you will say. Practice what you will say. Know what is most important and plan to say it first.

Again, be realistic about the kinds of responses you might get. If someone has abused you in the past it is unlikely that person will suddenly become sensitive to your needs. Disclosure of abuse usually disrupts a family system of denial. Often family members find the exposure so threatening that they turn the survivor into a scapegoat, denying or minimizing experiences or placing the blame on you. Various other family members call to berate you, telling you that you are wrong or even bad for saying what you are saying. They attempt to punish you by not being willing to talk to you, or they will no longer acknowledge you or your children. In extreme cases, some people have been taken out of wills. When other members of your family have also been abused and have repressed the abuse experience wanting to avoid feeling the pain around it, unearthing these feelings can be so threatening, or can imply such changes, that the family will reject the survivor altogether.

It is essential that you approach any confrontation by focusing on what you need to say rather than on any response you may get. Stay clear for yourself, your motivation, your needs. Don't be disappointed if you plan a scenario and it turns out different than you expected. If you can stay present with your needs, your feelings, you will be okay.

How Can I Share My Pain If My Parent Has Died?

Some readers feel as if they will miss an important part of recovery because they cannot share their thoughts and feelings with a significant person who has died. When they are working on early family issues, it is most commonly a parent who has died, but it can certainly be another family member, a partner, or friend with whom you would have desired sharing or confronting. These symbolic techniques provide that possibility.

When someone significant dies and hurt has been a part of your relationship to that person, there is usually much grief to be dealt with, grief of the past and for what will never be. When Elle's father died, she was confused about the intensity of her sense of loss—the physical pain that came with a very deep sadness and anger. Elle had never been close to her father. She thought she had accepted his indifference, his rejection of her. But when he died, she became profoundly aware of what she never had, nor would ever get from her father. She would never sit and enjoy his presence. She would never get his approval. She would never hear the words "I love you," words she was suddenly aware she longed to hear. In spite of the fact that she had been addressing the loss of a relationship with her father and had done a great amount of grief work, there was a depth of awareness that would only come after her father had died, which would lead to another layer of grief work. In her situation, the intensity or duration of the grief was deep, but not as great had she not done the previous work. For many, such as Elle, it is often the finality of the loss that pushes one to a final depth of grief and acceptance.

There are techniques, usually employed with therapists, which allow you to proceed in your process of wanting to speak to the deceased person. Letter writing, gestalt therapy, and psychodrama techniques can be very helpful. These techniques allow both you and this person to speak to each other. They are symbolic forms of communication, but highly therapeutic. Some people actually visit the person's grave and talk to the deceased. You can take a picture of the deceased, place it in a chair and tell them what you want to say. Some people need to say, "I am angry with you for . . ." or "I forgive you for . . ." or "I want you to know these things about me."

More than anything, you need to hear your recovery is about you—not whether or not a parent is living. It's about you and your relationship to life—and that includes coming to terms with family mortality.

Present-Day Relationships

By letting go of past and present pain, by creating healthier beliefs and developing new skills, you will create new ways of relating to family members with whom you were raised, and others you meet in your life—friends, coworkers, partners, husbands, wives, and children. Again, you have choices about whom you invite into your life and how you interact. Yet, you may still be confused about what creates a healthy relationship. One of the most important concepts in creating healthy relationships is understanding that relationships have different levels and purposes.

Some people are only in our lives, or we are only in theirs, to provide a practical service. For example, the bus driver's role is to see we are driven safely to a destination. The barber's role is to provide a satisfactory haircut. A coworker's role is to develop a relationship that allows the goals of the workplace to be met. The intimacy we develop with friends and partners offers a greater sense of meaning, purpose, and connectedness than our more casual and superficial relationships. I do not want to discount that we develop caring feelings toward those who work with us or provide services, but some people overwhelm others in an attempt to garner intimacy with all they meet. As a result, they often distance people in their unrealistic expectations, feel let down when others don't reciprocate, and have little intimacy with anyone. They find they have less time for those they've made commitments to and more with those whose relationship is more superficial.

Below I describe levels of adult relationships with the predominant purpose being:

Casual Involvement   Casual involvement occurs in relationships where people interact in a casual manner and have little or no commitment to one another.

Companion   Companionship involves two persons associating for the purpose of sharing a common activity. The activity is more important than the person and the person becomes interchangeable.

Friend   Friendship is where two people associate for the purpose of mutual support and enjoyment of each other. The person is most important. The activity is secondary.

Romantic   Romantic relationships are where friendship is shared with sensuality, passion, and sexuality. Romantic love is more than passion and sexuality. Passion and sexuality can be experienced in the context of casual involvement.

Committed   Committed relationship is where we mutually agree to do what we say we are going to do. We agree to work on whatever problems arise with a mutual trust of sincerity and intent.

While it is not always reality, it is healthiest for people to move through these levels as listed. Once a relationship has moved into a romantic or committed level, the couple continues to incorporate the previous levels into their daily lives. Committed relationships incorporate casual contact from the standpoint that superficial routine is a part of daily life. For people with a troubled childhood, it is important to learn that casual contact is not abandonment. The ability to move in and out of these levels will be incorporated into a committed relationship.

As well, there can certainly be intimate moments and experiences with strangers or companions. Those who experience natural crisis at the same time, those who are witness to a beautiful scene together, may connect in a highly intimate fashion. While such moments may be fleeting in time, they may affect us for life. Those times are seldom forgotten, yet it is with our close friends, partners, and family members that we experience our greatest ongoing intimacy.

Characteristics of a Healthy Relationship

We have gone through so much of our lives making assumptions or guessing about what is normal or appropriate in relationships. Many times we operate in a vacuum. As you read through the following characteristics of a healthy relationship, consider all your various relationships—with your parents, children, your partner, and your friends. There are degrees of difference in each relationship. You will set different physical boundaries defining how, when, and by whom you are touched; different emotional boundaries defining what you share and what you are willing to listen to; and different social boundaries defining where you will interact, with whom, and in what capacity. Yet, each characteristic applies to your relationships.

Respect
Respect is an attitude for which courtesy is an expression. My respect is an acceptance of who you are, your autonomy, the uniqueness of you.

Honesty
Honesty and open communication mean that people are free to be themselves.

"I have given up fear of rejection when I am less than perfect, when I am vulnerable, when it may mean you disagree with me. I can tell you my feelings, my thoughts, without fear of a major catastrophe." In order to be able to do this, we need to first be honest with ourselves so we can be honest with another. This also means we may need to learn healthy communication skills, the ability to speak for oneself, and the ability to listen.

Realistic Expectations

We need to be realistic about what we can offer another and what he or she can offer us. A past history of growing up with enmeshed boundaries, unrealistic expectations placed on us, or magical thinking on our part, can cause us to be very unrealistic of ourselves and others. Be aware that the other person is not going to be available or responsible for all of your needs. You are responsible for many of your needs, while different people together—friends, family, and partner—meet varying interpersonal needs.

Be cautious of someone trying to meet all of your needs at all times. It is likely that person is fearful of rejection, doesn't take responsibility for him- or herself, and hasn't developed a sense of self.

Trust

That means "I feel safe, psychologically and physically safe with you. I have no fears nor anxieties with respect to your treatment of me." For there to be trust, there needs to be consistency, predictability. To be trusted, a person has to demonstrate reliability, that he or she follows through with his or her intentions. Trust develops over time.

Autonomy

Intimacy is a sharing of autonomy. Real autonomy means each of us taking full responsibility for our own lives, for evolving into the best human being we can be. We are the fulfillers of our own life scripts and the exercisers of our own physical, emotional, and spiritual energies. With autonomy we have the ability to be clear about our own needs, being respectful to the boundaries and limits of others as well as ourselves. We are also able to honor the other person in his or her differences.

People need to be cautious in that sometimes autonomy passes for unbridled, unmitigated selfishness. "To hell with the rest of the world, I am going to get what I want when I want it because I am entitled to do what I please." That is not true. No one is entitled to get what he wants when he wants it from anyone. That is selfishness, intrusiveness, and greed.

A healthy relationship is not a power struggle between two rigidly autonomous beings, neither is it symbiotic. The two of you do not have to think and feel the same way about all things. We want to share ourselves without collapsing into one being. A healthy relationship grows in strength when there is shared autonomy.

Shared Power

A healthy relationship is about shared power, not control. Both people in the relationship are able to take initiative and to respond. They are able to stand side by side. There is a mutual give and take. The need to be right is relinquished. The idea of ownership is eliminated. There is mutuality and reciprocity in the relationship.

The notion of shared power with children is often a problem for parents. When children feel powerless, there are usually very negative consequences for both parents and children. While parents do need to operate from a position of authority and are responsible for providing healthy structure and boundaries, they can, nonetheless, provide children age-appropriate areas of mutual power sharing.

Tenderness

Tenderness is demonstrated with physical affection. This is the kind of nonsexual physical touching we all need to thrive. There is a nurturing touch that says, "I am here, you are not alone." "I offer my support." "Hello."

Tenderness is also expressed in words and attitude. It is so easy after being with people for long periods of time to let go of the little niceties we are so willing to offer those we don't know as well. It is easy over time to take our partners, parents, and even our friends for granted.

While the issue of safe sex is at the forefront of our thoughts today, the dynamics that create emotionally and spiritually safe sex also create physically safe sex. When you have an intimate adult-to-adult relationship built around spiritually and emotionally healthy guidelines, then physical sex becomes the culminating experience that binds you together.

Time

Relationships need time. When 150 couples in committed relationships, living together for more than four years, were asked how much time they spent with their partner each day, the answer was twenty-three minutes. Twenty-three minutes with the person each considered the most important to his or her life! People grow apart for many reasons, but for some it is as simple as getting caught up in other responsibilities and not taking time to "be" in a relationship. Valued relationships need time.

Long-term Commitment

To have a healthy relationship we need to pay attention to the dynamics of it and make a commitment to working on our part. We trust that if there are problems in our relationship, the two of us will work them out. We trust that when there are problems, it does not mean the relationship is over.

When we have spent so much of our life in a survivorship mode, it is very easy to think of the "worst-case scenario" when problems in our relationships arise. If the problem is with our partner, we may find ourselves automatically thinking of where we will go next, how we will support ourselves alone, and who else is or isn't "out there." We move into an all-or-nothing position, often beginning a defense against our incredible fear of rejection or abandonment. With our children, we may go into the "I'm a bad parent" orientation. While we may or may not physically abandon our children, we may fail to stay emotionally engaged. We forget we are their parent and succumb to a helpless role, leaving the child to sort out situations for him- or herself. Healthy parenting also requires a commitment to staying involved.

Commitment does not mean you stay in a relationship regardless of what may occur. As people change, relationships are renegotiated. Commitments are reinforced or lessened. When we make a commitment, we do what we can to make the relationship work, neither allowing ourselves to be abused, nor allowing ourselves to give up our integrity in the process.

While so many people are anxious to discover intimacy in a committed relationship, I don't want you to think that if you are not in a long-term, committed relationship there is something wrong with you. Not being in such a relationship may be the healthiest position you can be in at this time. When you are not in such a relationship, you can still work on the qualities that allow intimacy with friends, self, and a Higher Power.

Forgiveness

There has to be room for forgiveness in any relationship. Forgiveness does not mean selling your heart and soul or your integrity to have peace. It means remembering and letting go. It is a cleansing of your pain and anger. It means maintaining your integrity while being able to let go.

Charting the Characteristics of Your Relationships

Using these characteristics, the following are examples that may help you to reflect on how healthy you perceive yourself in specific relationships. On the continuum, 1 means the least and 10 means the most.

Shelia explored her relationship with her mother.

```
                              X        Respect
  1   2   3   4   5   6   7   8   9   10


                              X        Honesty
  1   2   3   4   5   6   7   8   9   10


                                  X    Realistic Expectations
  1   2   3   4   5   6   7   8   9   10


                          X            Trust
  1   2   3   4   5   6   7  .8  9   10


                                  X    Autonomy
  1   2   3   4   5   6   7   8   9   10
```

				X			X		Shared Power
1	2	3	4	5	6	7	8	9	10

			X						Tenderness
1	2	3	4	5	6	7	8	9	10

				X					Time
1	2	3	4	5	6	7	8	9	10

						X			Long-term Commitment
1	2	3	4	5	6	7	8	9	10

						X			Forgiveness
1	2	3	4	5	6	7	8	9	10

When Shelia worked this exercise, using her relationship with her mother as the focus, she was actually surprised all of her marks were in the high category. "I knew we had a healthy relationship, but it's not as close as this reflects." Remember, this reflects a healthy relationship, not necessarily closeness. Susan said, "Because of realistic expectations, I know what it is I can't get from my mother and that's emotional openness on her part. She's very closed. Yet, I can enjoy her and I do appreciate her tenacity. I stay actively engaged in having a relationship with her."

The following example is Nathan's reflection on how he sees himself to be relating with his seventeen-year-old son.

	X								Respect
1	2	3	4	5	6	7	8	9	10

		X							Honesty
1	2	3	4	5	6	7	8	9	10

		X							Realistic Expectations
1	2	3	4	5	6	7	8	9	10

X										Trust
1	2	3	4	5	6	7	8	9	10	

X										Autonomy
1	2	3	4	5	6	7	8	9	10	

		X								Shared Power
1	2	3	4	5	6	7	8	9	10	

X										Tenderness
1	2	3	4	5	6	7	8	9	10	

		X								Time
1	2	3	4	5	6	7	8	9	10	

					X					Long-term Commitment
1	2	3	4	5	6	7	8	9	10	

		X								Forgiveness
1	2	3	4	5	6	7	8	9	10	

Clearly, this relationship is struggling. It takes a lot of self-honesty to benefit from this exercise. Yet in doing so, Nathan realized how angry and disappointed he was with his son for not actively pursuing football and especially angry because of his son's sensitivity and orientation to music. In doing this Nathan recognized the crux to establishing a better relationship would be by working on allowing autonomy and respecting his son for his uniqueness and individuality. He knew when he became more honest with himself and then his son about his own image of being an athlete, and took responsibility for some past pain in his childhood, he would be more forgiving and more willing to spend time to solidify a commitment he was only now beginning to acknowledge.

Tracy chose to look at her relationship with her hairstylist because Tracy was not happy with how she was handling certain situations.

									X	Respect
1	2	3	4	5	6	7	8	9	10	

					X					Honesty
1	2	3	4	5	6	7	8	9	10	

					X					Realistic Expectations
1	2	3	4	5	6	7	8	9	10	

				N/A						Trust
1	2	3	4	5	6	7	8	9	10	

					X					Autonomy
1	2	3	4	5	6	7	8	9	10	

		X								Shared Power
1	2	3	4	5	6	7	8	9	10	

		X								Tenderness
1	2	3	4	5	6	7	8	9	10	

				N/A						Time
1	2	3	4	5	6	7	8	9	10	

					X					Long-term Commitment
1	2	3	4	5	6	7	8	9	10	

				N/A						Forgiveness
1	2	3	4	5	6	7	8	9	10	

In talking about her chart, Tracy had no difficulty respecting her hairstylist. But when Tracy was unhappy with the styling, she wouldn't tell the hairstylist. She wanted the hairstylist to somehow just know, to read her mind. Therefore, her realistic expectations were impaired. She was not owning her autonomy or taking her power; as a result, she was not feeling a strong commitment.

■■ *Take time to* explore your part of relationships in your life. In Appendix E, you will find a blank relationship form to chart a relationship that is important for you to explore.

Intimacy

In many families, intimacy was often built upon lies and distortions. Usually family members do not have the skills for intimacy. Even if they should, the nature of certain dysfunctions, such as addiction, interferes with such ability. As a result, people are very confused about the meaning of intimacy.

■■ *Describe what intimacy* means to you. How did you see it portrayed as a child? How is that still carried through in your behavior today?

- For Jackson, as a child, intimacy was when his mother sobbed on his shoulder because his father had wrecked the car one more time.
- For Holly, intimacy was when her father came home six hours late, had missed her school event, but came into her room to tell her he loved her.
- Blake said intimacy was sex. That was a time his mother wasn't crying and his father wasn't drinking.
- Victoria thought intimacy meant people being nice to each other. Being nice meant not arguing and not looking hostile.
- Odette said she thought intimacy was having a clean house.
- Robert said intimacy meant a loss of control.
- Lori said, "Intimacy means sharing with a friend or a partner. How can you do that when you have shame? When you feel inadequate? You can't talk about yourself honestly? You can't show your feelings? You can't trust?"

With perceptions as different as these, it is easy to see why people struggle with intimacy. Lori's questions are very significant. You will only be able to have the intimacy you so desire when you have first addressed your primary issues. You need to be able to separate your childhood fears from generalizing onto today's relationships. You need to develop a sense of healthy boundaries. You need to come to like yourself and appreciate who you are. You need to be willing to take risks. You need to know what it is you feel, what it is you need, and be able to communicate those feelings and needs. As you move forward in your recovery, your work will show itself in your relationships. All of the issues you have been working on contribute directly to a healthier way to be in a relationship.

As you commit to a relationship you are adding a room onto that home portrayed in Chapter Five. Will this be a continuation of the old beliefs, stories, secrecy? Or will your room have new furniture, fresh paint, and lots of windows and lighting?

We need to recognize there are differences in who we were in our past and who we are today. Today you are a person with many choices. You have the opportunity to develop clarity about what you value and like. You learn to identify your needs and feelings. You establish boundaries and set limits that create physical and psychological safety. You own the pain and shame of the past. By putting the pain in its proper perspective, you don't project it onto others or maintain shields of armor keeping people at a distance. You are developing the skills that will influence your choices of whom you do and do not invite into your life, allowing you much healthier ways of relating.

⤷ Intimacy is about being close. Intimacy is trusting another with who you are without the fear of rejection.

The different people we have relationships with are like characters in a play. Some will have minor roles and others starring roles. Some will help to codirect and coproduce our lives. They are all important to the overall play itself. We need to learn not to judge those who move in and out of the play, but to honor their appearance. Ultimately, we will look back on all of the people in our lives and realize we encountered them because they all had something to teach us.

Chapter Seven

Spirituality Is Something You Are

Forgiving, Loving, Finding Serenity

"Peace is not something you wish for. It is something you make, something you do, something you are and something you give away."

—Mother Teresa

"Faith and control cannot peacefully coexist."

—Claudia Black

When you set out on a new course in your life, the course of recovery, you are on a spiritual path. It is a path that leads to forgiving, accepting, loving, and finding serenity within yourself and with others. This spiritual path promises to lead you from aloneness and emptiness to a sense of connection and meaning in your life.

On this new journey, we are often involved in a process of spiritual growth before we recognize the spirituality of it. Looking back, the turning point came when we allowed ourselves to begin letting go of our fears and defenses to hear the truth:

There is another reality than the one I live. I want it.

This insight led us to learn more about the other reality and to learn more of the truth. The truth is that we are all human, both unique and ordinary, filled with dark and light. The truth is that all of our life experiences, whether admitted or denied, form the ground we stand on now. And the truth is that—in spite of our imperfections, our past and present pain, and the roles we've adapted to survive—in spite of all this, we now know that we are free to choose how we live our own lives. Realizing this, the victim's passive plea "Why me?" becomes a new, proactive question instead: "What can I do now?" This shift brings us to another turning point with another awareness:

ↄ I am responsible for the choices I make in my life.

When we accept our humanness and exercise our responsibility for making our own choices—for example, choosing what we do when we are angry, lonely, or sad—we are involved in a spiritual process. Our spirituality must be based on a vision that attends to our whole self and honors our whole experience, while at the same time acknowledges that we are accountable in the present for our own feelings, beliefs, and behaviors.

In *The Spirituality of Imperfection,* Ernest Kurtz writes that we have suffered *zerrissenheit,* or "torn-to-pieces-hood." Spirituality, as he describes it, is the healing process of "making whole." Spirituality helps us first to *see,* and then to *understand,* and eventually to *accept* the imperfection that lies at the core of our human *be*-ing.

Accepting our human limitations brings us inner peace. What a relief it is to put an end to the fight within ourselves. Also, as we find the permission to be the imperfect beings that we are, we become able to let others be who they are.

The experience of inner peace is foreign to those of us from shame-based families because there was so little peace and harmony in our lives. We didn't have models that projected unconditional love, acceptance, or gratitude. As a result, we came to believe that if we were anything less than perfect we were inferior and of little value. So, we sought perfection, believing it was our only avenue to acceptance and love. We were so hurt by the absence of the nurturing we needed to thrive that we have spent a great portion of our lives trying to make that unconditional love happen in the present, hoping somehow to make up for the past. Paradoxically, when we are willing to believe that we cannot change the past, then we become willing to let go of our pain.

In earlier chapters, we compared a family to a house with many rooms. Our growing-up years were lived in our parents' room, which was connected to their parents' room, and their siblings' room, and so on. The present is the room where we have lived our adult lives. A mixture of experiences has taken place in all these rooms. Some experiences were good, some caused a lot of pain. We need to realize that all families are imperfect, as all of us are imperfect people. To not understand or accept that truth will only hold us back in recovery. As Thomas Moore writes in *Care of the Soul*, "The sentimental image of family that we present publicly is a defense for the pain of proclaiming the family for what it is—a sometimes comforting, sometimes devastating house of life and memory."

To deny or disown any part of our experience leaves us dangerously incomplete and especially vulnerable to our shame. The lifeblood of shame is secrecy, fed by the dark fear of being found out. To grow toward wholeness in the context of our family home, we have to open all the doors and windows to let in air and light. Then, for us at last, healing will begin. Facing this truth, we reach another turning point:

ᕱ It is in the acceptance of all that was and is that our spirits become whole.

Bill Moyers described acceptance as wholeness and health in an interview on his book, *Healing and the Mind:* "Health is . . . a state of mind that recognizes the history of life, which includes moments of great delight and moments of deep sorrow. When we see all these parts of our being as connected, we come to terms with where we come from, who we are, and where we're going. Health is a whole."

In the process of becoming whole we may say we "have spirituality." But spirituality isn't an event or a possession. It's a way of living and being. Spirituality doesn't mean we never get hurt again, or that we are always smiling, always happy, never angry, and never scared. In part, spirituality means that when we are hurt or afraid we can respond without making matters worse. Also, as we change course and take steps on this spiritual road, we are able to enjoy the good feelings of being solidly balanced, open and unguarded, peaceful about the past and generally positive about how we are living in the present.

Spirituality and Control

Spirituality must also be based on the acceptance of another awareness:

    ↳   We are not "in control."

Sheldon Kopp says this another way: "No matter how well we may prepare, the moment belongs to God."

Accepting what we cannot control does not mean we give up all efforts to have order in our lives; we are not asked to thrive on chaos. We are asked only to give up the illusion that we can control what no one can. And, in accepting what we cannot control, we give up needlessly trying.

Because the whole notion of control is so clouded with anxiety and fear, let's try to clarify some issues: what we can and cannot control, our fears about losing control, and control versus surrender.

What We Can and Cannot Control

Some things are obviously out of our control—we can't make the sun come up or stop the rain. We can, however, build storm drains to channel the floods when the rain comes. In spite of our best efforts, sometimes the waters rise too high and houses are swept away. We are saddened by the loss, but we accept that we are not in control. We don't complicate our feelings with guilt or blame by thinking, *If only I had stopped the rain!*

In other aspects of our lives, control issues are easily confused. When we want something very much, we try very hard to get it or to make it happen. But, when we want something so much that we believe our lives depend on it, or our self-worth depends on it, then we believe we must make it happen. The belief "I must make it happen" implies that we *can* make it happen.

Control is often a confused factor in relationships. For instance, when someone believes, "I *must* have his or her love," it then seems logical to believe, "I must make him or her love me." Both beliefs are faulty—you will not die without the other's love and you can't make a person love you any more than you can stop the rain. However, when caught up in the emotion of wanting something so much, it is understandable that people get confused.

Parents are probably second only to lovers when it comes to being confused about what they can control. "My child must be good" or "My child must study hard" are beliefs that are followed by ". . . so I must make sure that happens." These outcomes can only be nurtured and encouraged, but not controlled.

> We can control going to bed. We cannot control sleeping.
> We can control reading. We cannot control understanding.
> We can control executing a play. We cannot control winning a game.
> We can control knowledge. We cannot control wisdom.

Learning to differentiate between what we can and cannot control is the first step to accepting our limitations. We are not God, we are not all-powerful—we are only humans and our power most definitely has limits.

Our Fears about Losing Control

As we consider giving up the idea of being in control, we are asking ourselves to have faith in something outside of our control. That in and of itself is a spiritual principle. Yet, being in control meant survival for so many of us. To manipulate people, places, and things brought order into our lives and offered the predictability we needed as children. When parents did not provide the structure that we needed, we attempted to provide it for ourselves. Being in control became a rigid form of protecting our self.

Therefore, recognizing that we need to let go of control to truly experience spirituality is often what makes people stop in their tracks.

Whether we grew up in a chaotic or a rigid family environment, the world was a scary place, so for survival we learned ways of reacting to our experiences and the people around us. We learned to shut down internally, to stop listening to our body, to our physical sensations and our emotions. These defenses blocked the natural tendency to be in tune with ourselves. We defended against our pain and shame externally with a variety of behaviors, ranging from compulsive busyness (work, hobbies, exercise) to social isolation, to the caretaking of others. Our responses to shame, ranging from control to perfectionism, from compulsive behaviors to chemical addiction—all are attempts to fill a spiritual void.

It is so important to have respect for doing what we needed to do to survive as children. Yet, today those old coping skills only get in our way. They create distance in our relationships. They interfere with enjoyment and fun.

Most important, control is a spiritual divider; it separates you from your spiritual self.

As we recognize life's open-endedness, we learn to be flexible and adaptable. In doing so, we are protected from the tendency to want to fix things, from our need to try to control the universe. This, in turn, offers us the opportunity to be at greater peace with the universe.

Control versus Surrender

Spirituality is a surrendering process, surrendering the illusion that we must have all the answers, that we must be in charge so we can hide our shame. By becoming aware of the reality about what we are able to control, and by facing our old fears of being out of control, we become willing to surrender. We surrender to our inability to change the past and to our powerlessness to control the future. That leaves us with real life in the present. Living in the here and now is another fundamental spiritual concept.

Once again, the absence of being in total control does not mean we are asked to thrive on chaos, that we cannot try to have order in our lives, at least some order some of the time. We need to remember that our need to control usually comes from a basis of fear. It is often a response to shame and operates from the motive that we need to try to control every aspect of ours and everyone else's lives.

There is also the part of spirituality where we humbly ask a Higher Power for guidance. Having faith, trusting in any person or concept outside of our own self when we were children so focused on surviving, seemed like suicide.

People in recovery are survivors of pain, and many of them sense that if they surrender control to a Higher Power, they will lose themselves in the process. To them, surrender feels like becoming vulnerable to boundary violations again, and also vulnerable in the sense of losing protection against their pain.

Growing up in a troubled family has often blocked our access to our spiritual self. Initially, our concept of a Higher Power, one whom we could supposedly trust, was learned from our interactions with our parents. Yet, these interactions most often taught us to not trust others, because even those closest to us could not be trusted. They made toxic decisions about the ways we were cared for and did not have our best interests at heart. Those experiences generalized to a belief that if a Higher Power did exist, no trust was possible there either.

In addition, when our sense of reality was continually invalidated, we learned not to trust the people who contradicted our internal messages. Even more devastating, we learned not to trust our own internal sensory experiences. Ultimately, we didn't even listen to the still, quiet voice from within.

When our earliest authorities, our parents, are incompetent, untrustworthy, or abusive, we learn not to respect or trust authority. For us, authority is to be feared. Authority, in our experience, uses power to control and /or punish. Obviously, we will resist the idea of surrendering to a Higher Power when it has a negative association with authority. To be open to believing in a Higher Power, we cannot conceive of the Higher Power as an authority that uses fear or control to influence.

�֍ ***Describe your concept*** of a Higher Power. Loving? Punishing? Indifferent? Other?

Spirituality and the Fear of Abandonment

Spirituality asks us to accept that there are many things we can't control. This acceptance includes surrendering our attachment to the outcome of those aspects of our lives we can't control. But what if everyone leaves us?

Can we surrender our attachment to that outcome, which might mean the possibility of abandonment? To find the answer, we must deal with our own fear of abandonment.

Originally, our fear of abandonment was fear of death. As infants, if food, love, and nurture weren't provided, we would be crippled or die. However, as adults, since we can provide the necessities for ourselves, our fear of abandonment is, in reality, the fear of pain. "If I am abandoned emotionally, the pain will be so bad I'll go crazy," or "If no one loves me, I am worthless. Being worthless is so painful I may as well die."

When we have these fears, as everyone does from time to time, the important thing to remember is that, as part of our spiritual process, we are learning to accept ourselves. Through self-acceptance we realize that our worth is not dependent on anyone else. This awareness brings us to another turning point:

   ⤷ I do not depend on others in order to accept myself.

This understanding is followed by another:

   ⤷ When people leave (abandon) me, it is not a judgment of my worth.

The truth is, any number of people may affirm us, but that will fall on deaf ears unless we accept and value ourselves.

We have come full circle. Our fear of abandonment can only be attended to and resolved by accepting ourselves. Conversely, if we don't accept ourselves and forgive our human limitations, we abandon ourselves.

Spirituality and Forgiveness

Forgiving Ourselves

So far, we have talked about accepting that which we can't control. However, accepting our imperfections sounds like a different matter. Imperfections mean that we don't always look as good as we want; we make mistakes that hurt others; we have secret fears that make us feel weak and secret desires that horrify us. How can we accept and forgive ourselves for these kinds of things?

To begin with, let's be clear that accountability and responsibility are not the same as forgiveness. We need to be accountable and responsible when we hurt others, and we need to make amends if possible. But then, we need to forgive ourselves for having made the mistake, for having blundered in our humanness again. While we may regret what happened, we can still forgive ourselves. Forgiving means not hanging on to the shame, which is only more destructive in the end.

People have so much trouble forgiving themselves because they can't answer the question, "Why should I be forgiven?" To start with, we might ask ourselves, "Why shouldn't I?" Often, this reveals the belief that somehow we're supposed to punish ourselves because we're guilty. This idea usually comes from our religious or family background, something we've learned and internalized. We're not born with an internal judge of our badness. We deserve to go back to that more loving place in our earliest development, instead of hanging on to the hurt, judgment, and negativity around us.

When we can't seem to budge our resistance to forgiving ourselves, another question to ask is, "What do I get out of maintaining the belief that I'm not okay or that I'm bad?" Also, it is humbling to forgive ourselves— maybe we don't feel okay being humble because humility is confused with being weak.

The opposite of "to forgive" is "to condemn." Whatever we condemn, we don't accept. In our acceptance and forgiveness, we learn to say, again and again:

I forgive myself for what I did to survive.
I forgive myself for continuing to make mistakes.

⬛ In what areas do you need to forgive yourself?

Forgiving Others

In accepting our own limitations we also learn to accept the imperfections of others. Forgiveness of others is a powerful manifestation of a spiritual connection. Many people on their course to family healing are able to understand why certain things occurred in the past, and in their recovery process they are able to come to a place of forgiveness in their heart. Others who experienced greater shame and pain at the hands of abusers struggle much more with forgiveness. People healing from family wounds become very confused about forgiveness, feeling there is a strong "should" attached to it, believing they "should" be able to forgive. This belief carries a message of good or bad and right or wrong. You are good if you forgive, bad if you do not. You are right if you forgive; you are wrong if you do not.

Other messages are implied when you believe you should forgive but don't feel ready to do so. One implication is that you are angry, and as such, you are bad and wrong. Another implication is that you are putting your priorities over others and that also is bad and wrong. We need to let go of our "shoulds." Forgiveness is not about being good or bad, right or wrong. It is about being true to yourself.

Whether or not you are able to forgive others is not the focus of treatment or recovery. Forgiveness is something you may ask for yourself; it is something you may pray to be able to give others. However, you may still be angry and hurt, and not ready to truly forgive. While it is not a goal of recovery, for many forgiveness is a gift that may come.

Only in knowing what forgiveness means to you can you put it into a healing perspective. The following are thoughts that I believe may be helpful to you as you sort through your feelings and come to terms with the role forgiveness has in your healing. By recognizing what forgiveness is *not*, it is more possible to see what forgiveness *is*.

What Forgiveness Is Not
Forgiveness is not forgetting.

We cannot forget what has happened, nor should we. Past experiences and even the pain have a great deal to teach us about not being victimized again and about not victimizing others.

Forgiveness is not condoning.

By forgiving the people who hurt us, we are not saying that what was done to us was acceptable, or unimportant, or "not so bad." It was important. It hurt, and it has made a difference in our lives.

Forgiveness is not absolution.

Forgiving others does not absolve them; it doesn't "erase" what they have done. They are still responsible for the harm they caused.

Forgiveness is not a form of self-sacrifice.

In forgiving, we are not swallowing our true feelings; forgiving does not mean playing martyr. There is a real difference between repressing a feeling and releasing a feeling.

Forgiveness doesn't mean we are never angry again about what occurred.

What happened to us was hurtful. It was not right; it was not fair. For that we may always feel anger. We have every reason and right to be angry. But we want to get to a point where our anger no longer interferes with how we care about ourselves or how we live our lives.

Forgiveness doesn't happen by making a one-time decision.

No matter how sincerely we want to let go of the past and move on with our life, we cannot just wave a magic wand and in one moment blithely make the past disappear. There is a process of grief work that we must walk through that allows forgiveness to occur.

What Forgiveness Is
Forgiveness is recognizing we no longer need our grudges and resentments, our hatred, our self-pity.

We do not need these negative emotions as excuses for getting less out of life than we want or deserve. We do not need them as a weapon to hurt those who hurt us or to keep other people from getting close enough to hurt us again.

Forgiveness is no longer wanting to punish the people who hurt us.

Realizing that we truly do not want to "even the score," forgiveness is the inner peace we feel when we stop trying to do so.

Forgiveness is no longer building an identity around something that happened to us in the past.

We realize that there is more to us than our past. The past is put into its proper perspective as one part of who we are in the present.

Forgiveness is what happens naturally as a result of confronting past painful experiences and healing old wounds.

Forgiveness is an internal process; it happens within.

Forgiveness is a moral right, not a moral obligation.

Forgiveness is remembering and letting go.

For most people, forgiveness is something that occurs gradually over time. As the work of recovery and healing takes place, anger and hurt are often replaced by forgiveness and deeply felt spiritual acceptance. With every tear that is shed and every cry of rage that is released, more room is opened for forgiveness to enter the heart.

Ultimately, it is your own powerful spirit that will heal you. Though we speak of body, mind, and emotions as distinct entities, they are inseparable and what affects one affects the others.

As you do the work of healing, forgiveness will naturally begin to manifest itself in your life by degrees. What is necessary for healing is a commitment to healing; forgiveness will then take care of itself.

For those of you who have been abused, the only forgiveness you need is forgiveness from yourself. You were a child. You did not have the power to respond any differently than you did. You were not bad or evil. Your body may have been violated; your emotions may have been repressed and turned inward; your view of yourself may be filled with fear, shame, grief, and rage. No matter what your experience has been, your spirit remains unspoiled and free and possesses a powerful force for healing.

✖ *Is there someone* you are wanting to forgive? Describe the behavior that was hurtful and how it has impacted you. What does forgiving mean to you?

Spirituality and Our Religious Upbringing

Unfortunately, our experiences with religion have very likely created conflict within us that interferes with our openness to a spiritual path. All too often we feel very alone and confused, seemingly betrayed by the only Higher Power we have ever known.

For most of us, that Higher Power was steeped in the definitions of a particular religion. Based on that religion, we were taught the Golden Rule to "Do unto others as you would have them do unto you." Be loving. Respect your parents. Be honest. Do not lie.

In many troubled families, however, children often found a contradiction between the religious teachings they were taught and what happened in their daily lives. Instead of respect, they heard verbal abuse. Instead of loving behavior, they saw one parent cause another intense anger or sadness. Instead of honesty, they witnessed their parents lie, or they were even told to lie for a family member under the guise of "protection." How many times did you and all the others in the family keep going to church, getting all dressed up, putting on your smiles, lying about why Mom or Dad weren't there? Did you find yourself saying they were sick, when Dad was too hung over to get out of bed, Mom didn't come home, or Mom was still bruised from Dad? How many times did you go home from church to neglect, abuse, or addiction kept hidden from the world?

Most children of troubled families truly believed in the Higher Power, as it was portrayed in their house of worship, but the contradiction of the religious messages with their family lives was too great for their continued commitment.

When you were growing up, how many times did you pray asking
- for Dad to come home, but he didn't;
- for Mom to be on time, but she was always late;
- for Dad to stop hitting Mom, but he wouldn't;

- for Dad to leave and never come back, but he stayed;
- for Mom to protect you, but she didn't;
- for Mom and Dad to be happy, but they never were;
- to take away the abuse, the neglect, the illnesses, the hurts, and disappointments, but they continued.

After feeling abandoned by our parents, feeling that our God had not answered our prayers was, for many of us, the ultimate abandonment experience.

> ✁ **Describe any contradictions** you experienced when growing up between religious teachings and your daily life. How has that impacted your religious or spiritual faith?

Spiritual Abuse

Spiritual pessimism and spiritual abuse were often created by religions that try to control us by generating fear that we are evil or bad, and that we may lose our souls. Great numbers of unsuspecting, trusting people have experienced spiritual abuse caused by harmful beliefs couched in a religious framework. These were beliefs that fueled fear, unworthiness, guilt, and shame. For people with such experiences, it will be necessary to review their religious beliefs to determine whether these have been spiritually nourishing or spiritually abusive.

Even more extreme are situations where parents use their religious beliefs or practices as a way to directly, or indirectly, control their children. Liz ultimately had to deal with the pain associated with her father always being away from home, attending to his parishioners, while she and five other children were left home alone with a raging alcoholic mother. When Liz was angry, she periodically yelled at her father in an effort to bring his attention to the pain going on at home and the fact he was needed at home by his children. Not willing to hear his daughter's pleas for help, she would be told to pray for forgiveness to the Almighty. Being angry was perceived as a sin. All painful feelings, particularly anger, were seen as being separate from God. To express that anger at an authority was a greater sin. To put your needs ahead of others (Dad's parishioners) was a higher sin.

In Liz's case, religious beliefs were used to induce guilt and shame, and in so doing, indirectly controlled her life. In Nates' experience, the issue of control was very direct. Nate was forced to read the Old Testament repeatedly and then was quizzed by either his mother or father before being able to spend time with friends. Nate was told it was the Bible that would dispense rewards. As a consequence, it was the Bible that was to become his punishing stick.

These cases of abuse associated with religion were not really religious practices advocated by a church's doctrine. These were abuses by very hurtful, frightened, shameful, controlling adults who used aspects of their religion to control and manipulate young children. Yet, when these same children become adults, it is often the religious doctrine they are angry with, not the people who framed it to suit their purpose.

Without addressing their past spiritual abuses, they will continue to struggle with contradictory experiences. It is important to sort out "the messenger from the message." It is important to develop a relationship with a doctrine whose tenets don't foster punishment and shame. We do not deserve to live in fear of a wrathful and punishing God, but to believe in the good of all, and that includes ourselves.

Believing that our prayers were not heard or, even worse, believing that our prayerful pleas for help were ignored, created spiritual conflict within us. Having our parents or those "of the church" use religious beliefs or practices to punish, humiliate, or control us also leads to spiritual conflict. We feel abandoned by our parents, possibly by our church, and as we said earlier, ultimately abandoned by God. In addition to feeling abandoned and hurt, we may be angry with our parents, the church, and also with God. Just owning the possibility that you are angry with God may be very frightening.

If you are angry, you need to acknowledge and externalize your anger. This is often the first step in clearing the way to a spiritual path that will help you to come to peace with your past. A helpful technique for expressing your anger and rage is to write a letter to God (your Higher Being). In your letter, tell your Higher Being why you are angry. People sometimes feel uncomfortable doing this, but remember that when you release pent-up anger and rage, relief and reconciliation will follow. It is easier to do this exercise when you have come to believe that your Higher Power is forgiving and loving.

✖ *While religion and* spirituality are not necessarily one and the same, it may be helpful to explore your childhood history, to help understand how your experiences with religion may be impacting your concept of spirituality. Here are some questions to give thought to, to write or talk to someone about.

1. Were you forced to attend a specific house of worship as a child, or otherwise participate in religious practices? If your involvement ended, what made you stop? If you didn't attend any type of faith-based house of worship, how was that decision made?
2. If you were involved in a church, synagogue, mosque, or other religious group, describe your experience. Fun, scary, boring, hopeful, meaningful? Other?
3. Were there any particular rituals or ceremonies that were of special value or significance for you? What were they? How were they special?
4. Looking back at your early religious influence, what aspects were positive that are still with you today? Are there any negative influences that are still with you?

It is not uncommon for people to return (or if they didn't leave it, to engage more positively) to the faith and church of their youth, while many others choose a different faith or church. Some decide to follow a guru. Others decide to follow the Earth Religions. Many people practice twelve-step concepts. It has been reported that the twelve-step program, beginning with Alcoholics Anonymous in 1935, is the largest spiritual (not religious) movement in the United States. Many combine these philosophies and practices. In recovery, every spiritual door is open.

Again, for the sake of clarity, religion is a set of beliefs that follows from a central belief in God or a Higher Power, and a set of practices that arises out of those beliefs. Religion can be a bridge to the spiritual. However, organized religion does not necessarily include spirituality. Spirituality is not a framework for a set of beliefs, although spirituality may be an integral part of a religion.

Spirituality and the Spirit of Our Inner Child

Children are authentic, and spirituality is about being authentic in the way we exist. Children are naturally present in the moment. They are in tune with and entranced by the mysterious life that they embody. Children have a natural affinity for the earth, seen by their sitting on the ground, rolling down hills, etc. They feel a connectedness to the elements—the wind, the sky, animals, the trees. Until taught otherwise, children believe the world is their friend. They are curious and receptive to its ever-changing flow of events. Our earliest spiritual experiences were all natural.

The authentic, uncensored, connected child is the Natural Child, the Inner Child who still lives within each of us. Our Inner Child consists of our intuitiveness, spontaneity, our vitality. It is the part of us that is naturally open and trusting until it learns to shut down for self-protection. It is emotionally expressive until it is criticized. It is playful until its spirit is crushed for being exuberant. It is creative until ridiculed. We often bury our Inner Child, ignore it, distort it, or medicate it, but our Inner Child is our spirit that remains with us. When we become disconnected from our Inner Child, we lose much of the mystery and magic of life. We lose the delight of intimacy; we lose our spiritual self.

Another way to describe our Inner Child is to recognize it as the cognitive framework for our vulnerable self. Also, it is that part of our self that knows what we feel and what we need. Referring to our vulnerable self as our Inner Child is a way to access or get in touch with this knowing.

In order to get in touch with our Inner Child we sometimes have to go back and undo messages that obscure our most tender, deepest feelings. We have to get in touch with those feelings in order to open up to our spirit within. Just as a dark, secret room in our family house is a metaphor for a shameful secret, so is our Inner Child a metaphor for the softest, most natural feelings we hold inside. For the life-breath of spirituality to move throughout our lives, we must open all the avenues to all the protected and vulnerable places within us; we must open up and connect with our Inner Child.

When you have a hard time accessing your Inner Child, think about something or someone for whom you have unconditional love: your child or your pet. Using your dog as an example, when he is playful, do you think of calling him foolish? When he barks in fear, do you believe he is stupid or cowardly for being afraid? Can you tap into the sense that, for your pet, there are no "shoulds" or "shouldn'ts" for its feelings and behaviors? Therefore, your pet lives free of judgment or shame. Now, are you willing to offer yourself that same freedom?

In doing Inner Child work, you will come to identify several different aspects of your Inner Child. Often there is the Victim Child, who says, "I am helpless! I need someone else to do it for me." Or the Frightened Child, who says, "Go away! I don't need you!" Or the Angry Child, who says, "Where have you been? You left me all alone! I don't want you now!" It can be helpful to attach different names to the different experiences of our vulnerable self. In doing so, it gives us a framework to get in touch with how vulnerable we have been and often still are.

As you come to know different aspects of your Inner Child, try to recognize that these different aspects are protectors of the innocent Natural Child. When your Natural Child was not being nurtured, heard, and supported, you created other aspects of your Inner Child that offered a form of protection to your true self. Therefore, as you are doing your healing work, it is only natural that you will uncover the pain of the Wounded Child. Much of what you hear from your inner self is the voice of the abandoned Wounded Child—his or her fear, anger, grief, and pain. You may have to spend months being present for your Wounded Child in a loving way before some of the inner pain begins to heal. As that pain begins to melt away, your protector selves will begin to relax, which in turn will clear the way for the Natural Child to emerge.

Songwriter and singer Lauren Michaels reflects the spirit of the child in the song, "A Child Knows."

> A child knows, a child knows . . .
> A child knows, a child knows.
> A child hears the wind sing;
> A child knows the earth's a living thing.
>
> A child sees the leaves dance;
> A child knows, there is no second chance.
> Live right now, live right now.

> Dance right now, sing right now.
> Raise your hands and your voice to the wonder of it all.

Healing is about learning to connect with and to love our natural self. Rejecting the child within us is another way to reject ourselves and to abandon the care of our inner spirit.

■ *The following is* a guided imagery reflection. Set aside ten to fifteen minutes and allow yourself to be a quiet place, without possible interruptions. If you have soft music you enjoy, you may want to play it in the background. Slowly read the following:

Find a comfortable position and uncross your arms and legs. Take a deep breath in . . . and out. Take another deep breath in . . . and out.

As you breathe slowly and deeply, begin to relax your body, allowing the tension to dissolve . . . the worries of the day, the stresses of decisions moving out of your body.

Take a deep breath in . . . and out.

If there are any places in your body that still feel tight or tense, where you are holding energy you don't need, put your awareness into those places . . . breathe into them. As you breathe out, imagine the tension or the excess energy releasing and dissolving away so that your entire body feels deeply relaxed.

Slowly, breathe in . . . and out.

Think of a place you can go in your mind—a magical place, a special place just for you. Now imagine yourself in that place. For some it is a pond out in the woods, for others it is a rock perched on the sand at the beach, or it may be a special place in your home or yard.

Wherever it is, it is your place to go there now.

Relaxed, imagine yourself slowly, ever so gently becoming engulfed in waves of color. Pinks . . . blues . . . greens . . . whites . . . purples . . . oranges. Colors of love. Colors of safety. Colors of nurturance. These colors may be soft, pastel, rich, and intense. Whatever the colors, they feel loving and safe.

Continue to breathe deeply in . . . and out.

Now, in your special place full of loving, safe colors, be with these words:

> *You are very special.*

> *You may never have had the opportunity to believe in your specialness.*

> *You may believe in it today.*

> *Today, you may respond with the vulnerability of your inner child but the strength of your adult.*

> *Feelings are to be listened to; they are cues and signals that indicate where you are and what you need.*

> *Mistakes are a sign of growing; remember to be gentle with yourself.*

> *Recovery is accepting yourself for who you are, no longer waiting for others to define or approve of you.*

> *You can't live your life by walking someone else's path.*

> *Trust in yourself. Your perceptions are far more accurate that what you have been willing to believe.*

> *Your strengths are more powerful than your vulnerabilities.*

> *Believe in your right to happiness, respect, and dignity.*

It is in faith that you will find the strength to survive times of great fear and sadness.

The truth begins with you, your truth.

Be with those words in your magical place of color. Know that you may return to that place any time you choose. Take a slow deep breath in . . . and out. When you are ready, reorient and make eye contact with your surroundings.

Practicing Spirituality

Spirituality acknowledges and does homage to the spark of divinity within each of us; it is an approach to life, an attitude. As we grow spiritually, we learn to trust that life will continue to unfold as it must. We will remain spiritually whole, grounded in our authenticity, and centered in our openness to learning. To grow spiritually we must walk the walk. Practicing spirituality means that we

- do the footwork;
- be present, be in the here and now;
- stay attuned to our inner guidance;
- be authentic;
- put forth the effort;
- let go of the attachment to the results; and,
- believe in the divine guidance and choice it offers.

Spirituality must be lived, practiced consistently, and acted on consciously. The spiritual path is a commitment to personal transformation, to service, and to not harming others. This commitment shows itself most clearly in a person's attitude toward life. Our personal spirituality is a blend of our intent to be authentic and our openness to our intuition. From this foundation follows a willingness to trust, to be tolerant and gentle, and a willingness to continue learning from life.

The practice of spirituality embraces gratitude as an attitude that is both a measure of our happiness and a reminder to find our happiness. It is being grateful for what we do have, instead of regretting what we do not have. We learn tolerance and acceptance of both likenesses and differences. It recognizes and understands that we all struggle with the same fears and sorrows, and we all do the best we can with what we have.

Practicing spirituality in our lives finds us taking time daily to honor our humanness, to appreciate the universe, and to give and share with others. Selfless service is a spiritual practice, but must be distinguished from the guilty need to rescue. Selfless service, or service from the self, comes not from need, but from compassion. In spiritual practice, what we offer to others is given freely and spontaneously. It comes from our heart, without expectation of return. In service, we feel the truth that to give is to receive. Spirituality is an ability to accept love, as well as the capacity to give love. It is an instinctive empathy, an act of kindness, generosity, and intuitive thoughtfulness.

Recovery changes the course of our search for serenity from the outer world to the inner one. Our true self cannot be discovered from the outside. Our being can only be discovered in the silence of our inner life. We access our real identity when our mind becomes quiet and we are fully conscious and present in the moment.

A common symptom of modern life is that there is no time for thought, or even for letting the impressions of a day sink in. Yet even the simplest act of pausing offers a period of non-doing that is essential nourishment of the spirit. Washing dishes is no less an invitation to a holy moment than is a sunset. Listening to friends, playing with children, stroking our pets, sharing from the heart, these are ways that we naturally center. Similar to pausing, and just as important in the care of the spirit, is the practice of taking time out. The spirit basks in the extended sense of time. Setting aside time is the spiritual practice that supports all other spiritual works.

The world is filled with noise and distractions, from television to social chatter to unbidden thoughts. It is important to develop a process of turning off the external noise and tuning in the internal voice, the still quiet voice within. There is no one right way to practice this. You might find that setting aside time at sunset to watch the changing colors, to feel the changing atmosphere, to hear the sounds at dusk and breathe in tune with the experience will take you right into that quiet place inside where you commune with that which is holy.

Spiritual development requires spiritual practice, just as the person who wants to be physically fit must exercise. Without the workouts nothing happens. If you set your course toward inner calm and peace of mind, daily spiritual practice is necessary.

Spirituality is a process of going inward to the part of yourself that is connected to the larger context. Some of the spiritual practices to connect with your inner life are

- prayer
- meditation
- practice of silence/quietness
- guided imagery
- living a thought-*full* life

As you engage in spiritual practice, the location, the sounds, the time, the use of materials often become significant and meaningful parts of your ritual. Many people include rituals involving deep breathing and relaxation. By definition, spirituality is derived from the Latin word *spiritus,* which means the act of breathing. Breathing allows you to be open within your own body, to go "inside." Once your physical body is relaxed, it is necessary to relax your mind and let go of thoughts and worries.

Prayer is common in the church, the ashram, or the temple. It is also an important part of spiritual practice throughout the day. Some people have a favorite meditation book and include reading from it during times of prayer. Some people get on their knees; others have a sitting area where they are surrounded by favorite objects, photographs, and plants. Prayer and/or meditation is something you can do while sitting in your living room, lying in your bed, walking along the beach, or jogging in the park. Both prayer and meditation are practices that nurture and develop our connection to self and spirit. Prayer is an act that puts us in touch with a power greater than all else.

For many people, particularly those who have used keeping busy as a form of self-protection, the idea of meditation is particularly frightening. The idea of doing what appears to be nothing or just being is difficult to comprehend. Yet, it is meditation that allows you to completely stop, to let go of thoughts about the immediate past or future, and simply focus on being in the here and now.

> ❖ *Describe your personal* orientation toward spiritual practice. What behaviors or thoughts interfere with your daily commitment to a spiritual life? What do you need to support yourself in your spiritual practice? Are there other spiritual practices you would like to explore?

Spirituality, the Turning Point to a New Course

For so many of us, our entire lives have been about reacting, surviving, and being vigilant to the outside forces. We want and we deserve the other reality. Many of us are used to being in control and want recovery right now, so we try to skip over the emotional work and go directly to the promised spiritual realm. Others of us attempt to find inner peace and harmony from an intellectual understanding, or we do volunteer work to demonstrate our spiritual intent. While any sincere effort can be extremely valuable, we cannot singularly will ourselves to a higher plane. We cannot skip the steps in recovery. We cannot be spiritual people unless we do the necessary work. Part of the work on ourselves is to understand our past and present relationship with a Higher Power. We can do that only when we take time out to listen to our own internal processes. When we can hear our heart and soul, we experience our spiritual truth.

Becoming whole requires a journey into and through the darkness of the wounds of childhood and healing our child within. When we begin to experience the world as less frightening, we know we can take care of ourselves; we know we have the inner resources to make it; we do not have to live in hyper-vigilance any longer. We can say no to our shame. Doing these things, we move beyond the confines of the past on to a course of spirituality in the present.

When we accept that we cannot be the Higher Power ourselves, it is the turning point of our recovery. When we come to believe that the Higher

Power is all around us and also within us, that is the turning point of our spirituality.

Some of us have experienced these turning points through our houses of worship. Others of us find it in nature, in song, or the power of a group.

But God is always present in the heart.
Look within.

↳ Turning Points to Recovery

- There is another reality than the one I live. I want it.
- I am willing to take some risks to have it.
- If you have pain, you deserve to heal.
- If you have anger or guilt from the past, you deserve to heal.
- If you are protecting yourself from past pain in ways that are causing you even more pain in the present, you deserve to heal.
- The pain we feel is not only from the past, but also from the past-driven present.
- We were powerless in the past, but we are not powerless in the present.
- We are not our pain.
- Our pain is our responsibility.
- What we do about our pain is a choice we make.
- To say, "I did not learn this basic skill, and I need to know it," is a turning point.
- Recovery isn't changing who you are. It is letting go of who you are not.
- Recovery is learning the numbers two through nine.
- By recognizing that you are in the process of recovery, you are beginning to shine your own light.
- You deserve to begin rebuilding your life in a new direction.
- Learning to love yourself does not mean you love others less. Instead, it frees you to love them more.

- The awareness that now you can choose to be free from the secret is a turning point.
- A turning point will come when you can identify a safe way to share the secret.
- The awareness of your own role is a turning point.
- The awareness that we have adopted a protective role is a turning point.
- The awareness that we no longer need that role to survive is a turning point.
- The turning point in your relationship is the awareness that your growth is not about getting other people to change.
- You are not a coward if you choose not to confront face-to-face.
- Intimacy is about being close. Intimacy is trusting another with who you are without the fear of rejection.
- I am responsible for the choices I make in my life.
- It is in the acceptance of all that was and is that our spirits become whole.
- We are not "in control."
- I do not depend on others in order to accept myself.
- When people leave (abandon) me, it is not a judgment of my worth.

God is always present in the heart. Look within.

Special thanks to

Lauren Michaels, Bonnie Hesse, and Sandi Klein who were all pivotal to the earlier edition of *Changing Course*. Their feedback, proofing, editing, and passion for this manuscript made it possible.

Stuart Smith, Valerie Killeen, Patrick Hughes, John Davis, and Nancy Schenck at Central Recovery Press for honoring my work.

Appendices

Appendix A
Personal Loss Graph for Early Years

Appendix B
Loss Graph Exercise (Early Years)
These graphs relate specifically to losses in the early years.
The following graphs are examples to help you begin your own.

Appendix C
Personal Loss Graph for Adult Years

Appendix D
Loss Graph Exercise (Adult Years)
These graphs relate specifically to losses in adult years.
The following graphs are examples to help you begin your own.

Appendix E
Charting Your Relationships

Personal Loss Graph for Early Years

Loss
Events Age
Unattended Feelings

Abandonment:

Loss Conditions in Family:

- To begin your loss graph, note the loss events that immediately come to your mind without trying to judge whether or not you are still affected.

- Record your age and any feelings you remember having had at the time.

- Next, note losses you remember related to chronic conditions within your family, such as those which resulted in your feelings of inadequacy, shame, fear, loss of control, loss of innocence, loss of childhood. Sometimes these losses are due to addiction and abuse; many times they are not, but they are nonetheless painful. If you are unable to easily identify family conditions, you may find it helpful to ask: "What was I afraid of? Ashamed of?" Don't force this. Referring to chapter 1, pages 1–16 may be helpful.

Loss Graph Exercise (Early Years) Libby

Loss	Grandmother	Best friend	Parents	Family dog
Events Age	died 7	moved 10	divorce 11	died 15
Unattended Feelings	sad scared	sad lonely unloved	guilty angry	sad alone

Loss Conditions in Family:
Mother: depressed
Mother: always in bed
Father: always at work

Abandonment Experiences/Feelings:
Guilty for mother's crying
Angry because alone
No one came to my school events
Afraid to bring friends home
Guilty, believing I'm at fault
Unloved

Libby's loss events can be considered fairly common. However, because of the loss conditions in her family, with her parents being unavailable to comfort her and help her feel secure and safe, her abandonment experiences left her with feelings of low self-worth.

Loss Graph Exercise (Early Years) Tim

Loss	Involved in a car accident Brother died Tim broke arm and leg Missed half of school year	Changed to a new junior high	Afghanistan combat service
Events Age	7	12	18 to 21
Unattended Feelings	terror sadness	scared angry	fear powerlessness

Loss Conditions in Family:
Father: rager
Father: alcoholic
Mother: martyr
Mother: continually blamed father for accident
Parents: constantly idealized deceased brother

Abandonment Experiences/Feelings:
Never good enough compared to brother
Worthlessness
Chronic fear of dying (not protected by parents)
Never a sense of safety from war experiences

Tim's losses may have caused deeper wounds than Libby's, especially his brother's death and his combat exposure in Afghanistan. Still, if he'd had family support and love, he would have had an opportunity to attend to and grieve his pain. But Tim also had an overlay of family loss conditions, leaving him even more helpless to attend to his feelings. Consequently, his pain was heightened by his feelings of fear, powerlessness, and inadequacy.

Personal Loss Graph for Adult Years

Loss
Events Age
Unattended Feelings

Loss Conditions in Family: **Abandonment:**

_____   _____

_____   _____

_____   _____

_____

- To begin your loss graph, record the loss events you experienced as an adult, your age at the time, and the feelings that you remember having when the losses occurred.

- Also, record loss conditions and abandonment experiences and feelings that have been a part of your adult life. When you create this loss graph, remember that you are trying to record your adult experiences—not those you remember having happened when you were a child.

- Loss conditions are different from loss events and abandonment experiences. A condition is a state that exists over time, so adult loss conditions may very likely include unresolved childhood conditions. If your childhood losses are still creating pain for you in the present, then this is a very real condition in your adult life.

Loss Graph Exercise (Adult Years) Libby

Loss Events Age	Miscarriage 21	Divorce 23	Left college prematurely due to stress 24	Aware of marital infidelity 36	Lost job promotion 38
Unattended Feelings	despair	despair fear	sad	anger frightened insecure	despair

Loss Conditions in Family:
Unresolved childhood pain
Emotionally abusive partner
Compulsive overeater

Abandonment Experiences/Feelings:
Inadequate
Frightened
Sad
Ashamed
Anger

Libby carried into adulthood the unresolved feelings of her childhood. Added to this was the pain of adult loss events, pain that she had not yet learned to work through. The feelings were there but she was unable to attend to them. In addition, she chose a partner that fueled her sense of shame and abandonment. Her compulsive overeating only heightened the accumulation of these feelings. Except for her compulsive overeating, most people saw Libby as a happily married mother of two daughters who worked as a medical records specialist in a community hospital. Libby's loss graph, however, offers a strong visual record of pain, a striking contrast to her public image.

Loss Graph Exercise (Adult Years) Tim

Loss	Engagement	Loses job	Son, 6 years old
Events Age	24	26	36
Loss	broken	Loses job	diagnosed with cancer
Unattended Feelings	angry	angry	frightened
	sad	frightened	sad
	lonely		

Loss Conditions in Family:

Unresolved childhood and Afghanistan combat pain Wife
depressed
Chronic conflict around child's loss of health

Abandonment Experiences/Feelings:

Sadness
Fear
Futility

Like Libby, Tim never worked through the pain of major loss events in his youth, such as his brother's death and his own military service. Consequently, as an adult, Tim carried pain from the past, compounded by severe loss conditions in his own family, especially his son's serious illness. At the age of thirty-six, Tim struggled to present himself to the world as a man who loved his family and enjoyed his work as a media technician at a local television station. But because Tim never learned the emotional skills to heal his pain, his loss graph clearly depicts a heavy burden of past and present pain..

Charting Your Relationships

Respect

1 2 3 4 5 6 7 8 9 10

Honesty

1 2 3 4 5 6 7 8 9 10

Realistic Expectations

1 2 3 4 5 6 7 8 9 10

Trust

1 2 3 4 5 6 7 8 9 10

Autonomy

1 2 3 4 5 6 7 8 9 10

Shared Power

1 2 3 4 5 6 7 8 9 10

Tenderness

1 2 3 4 5 6 7 8 9 10

Time

1 2 3 4 5 6 7 8 9 10

Long-term Commitment

1 2 3 4 5 6 7 8 9 10

Forgiveness

1 2 3 4 5 6 7 8 9 10

About the Author

Claudia Black, PhD is a renowned author and trainer internationally recognized for her pioneering and contemporary work with family systems, addictive disorders, and traumatic stress. Her writings and teachings have become a standard in the field of addiction. She is a Senior Fellow and the Clinical Architect of the Claudia Black Young Adult Center at The Meadows Treatment Center in Arizona. She is a cofounder on the advisory board for the National Association for Children of Addiction and the advisory council of Camp Mariposa, a part of the Eluna Network. She is the author of numerous books including *Unspoken Legacy: Addressing the Impact of Trauma and Addiction within the Family*, *Repeat After Me: A Workbook for Adult Children Overcoming Dysfunctional Family Systems*, and *Intimate Treason: Healing the Trauma for Partners Confronting Sex Addiction*.

Also Available by Claudia Black

Claudia Black is the author of over fifteen books, all available via Central Recovery Press. See the Claudia Black Library at CentralRecoveryPress.com for a full list and descriptions of her books, CDs, and videos.

Books

Deceived	9781949481082
Depression Strategies	9781949481327
Family Strategies	9781942094920
A Hole in the Sidewalk	9781942094739
Intimate Treason	9781936290932
It Will Never Happen to Me	9781949481402
My Dad Loves Me, My Dad Has a Disease	9781942094753
Repeat after Me	9781942094777
Straight Talk	9781949481143
The Truth Begins with You	9781936290611
Unspoken Legacy	9781942094562

CDs/DVDs

A Time for Healing - CD	705105051130
Addiction in the Family - DVD	705105051932
Anger - DVD	705105051833
Children of Denial - DVD	705105052137
Double Jeopardy - DVD	705105052236
Emotional Baggage - CD	705105051239
Imageries - CD	705105051338
Issues of Recovery - DVD	705105052335
Legacy of Addiction, The - DVD	705105052434
Letting Go Imageries - CD	705105051437
Putting the Past Behind - CD	705105051536
Relapse - DVD	705105052533
Trauma in the Addicted Family - CD	705105051635
Triggering Effect - DVD	705105052632
Triggers - CD	705105051734
What Do I Say to My Kids - DVD	705105052731

Printed in the USA
CPSIA information can be obtained
at www.ICGtesting.com
JSHW022330140824
68134JS00019B/1393